Dark psychology

The Ultimate Guide to Decode Body Language,
Analyze People, Against Deception, Mind control,
Manipulation, Evade Brainwashing, and More

Abraham Copeland

© **Copyright 2020 - All rights reserved.**

The content contained within this book may not be reproduced, duplicated or transmitted without direct written permission from the author or the publisher.

Under no circumstances will any blame or legal responsibility be held against the publisher, or author, for any damages, reparation, or monetary loss due to the information contained within this book. Either directly or indirectly.

Legal Notice:

This book is copyright protected. This book is only for personal use. You cannot amend, distribute, sell, use, quote or paraphrase any part, or the content within this book, without the consent of the author or publisher.

Disclaimer Notice:

Please note the information contained within this document is for educational and entertainment purposes only. All effort has been executed to present accurate, up to date, and reliable, complete information. No warranties of any kind are declared or implied. Readers acknowledge that the author is not engaging in the rendering of legal, financial, medical or professional advice. The content within this book has been derived from various sources. Please consult a licensed professional before attempting any techniques outlined in this book.

By reading this document, the reader agrees that under no circumstances is the author responsible for any losses, direct or indirect, which are incurred as a result of the use of information contained within this document, including, but not limited to—errors, omissions, or inaccuracies.

Table of Contents

Analyze People 5

    Chapter 1. Introduction 7

    Chapter 2. Introduction to Human Behavior Psychology 13

    Chapter 3. Why to Analyze a Person? 21

    Chapter 4. Characteristics, Different Forms of Non-Verbal Communication 29

    Chapter 5. Rules for Accurate Reading 33

    Chapter 6. Under Standing Body Language 41

    Chapter 7. Analysis of People through Words 47

    Chapter 8. Detecting Lies and Deception 51

    Chapter 9. Genetic Information to Place People in Different Temperaments of the Personality 55

    Chapter 10. Verbal Cues 65

    Chapter 11. Highest Quality "Tells"—Facial Expressions 75

    Chapter 12. What Are They Really Saying? 83

    Chapter 13. How to Spot a Lie—Key Behavior That Indicates Deception? 91

    Chapter 14. How to Seduce with Your Body Language and Verbal Communication 103

    Chapter 15. Analyzing People via Their Verbal Statements 115

    Chapter 16. Signs of Confidence and Lack of Confidence 117

    Chapter 17. Persuasion 123

Chapter 18. Conclusion 131

Manipulation **135**

Chapter 1. Introduction 137

Chapter 2. The Foundations of Manipulation 139

Chapter 3. What Makes People Chat Without Thinking? 145

Chapter 4. Manipulation of the Mind Through NLP 149

Chapter 5. Mental Control with NLP for Love and Relationships
.... 161

Chapter 6. Advanced Manipulation Methods: Love Bombing, Foot-In-The-Door, NLP Mirroring 171

Chapter 7. List of Errors That Can Make You Vulnerable to Manipulation 183

Chapter 8. Skills to Be Developed to Become a Manipulator 195

Chapter 9. Manipulation Rules/Techniques 211

Chapter 10. Understand Manipulation Techniques and Act Accordingly 215

Chapter 11. Manipulation and Moral Question: Why Is Manipulation Important in Life 221

Chapter 12. Psychological Manipulation Through Words 231

Chapter 13. 9 Brilliant Strategies for Seducing A Person Using Manipulation 241

Chapter 14. Solutions to Overcome Manipulation 253

Chapter 15. Conclusion 261

Analyze People

Effective guide on how to analyze body language and use behavioral techniques of dark psychology to read into people's minds and defend themselves from manipulation and deception

Chapter 1. Introduction

The ability to analyze people impacts your relationship with them. When you develop a greater understanding of how someone feels or tailor your message/ communication pattern to make sure it is received as intended. Learning about reading and analyzing people helps you understand what clues you should be watching out for a while communicating with people. What are the things you should be carefully listening to? What are the typical signs that indicate how someone thinks or feels? How can you spot when someone is lying? How can you sense deception and dishonesty?

Glossies and periodicals such as Cosmo, GQ, and Psychology Today have a huge number of pages devoted to pop quizzes and pop psychology features such as "Ten Ways to Tell If a Man is Really into You" or "Tell-Tale Signs Your Kids Are Lying to You: Watch Out for Their Feet Position to Know the Truth." Pop psychology has partially ruined the analyzing people game, by converting it into a non-serious, entertaining pursuit, which would be good if it wasn't so inaccurate.

In a more practical sense, this isn't how it works. You can't tell if a man is into you or not based on the shape of his eyebrows when he looks at you. Similarly, lying children can't be called out by looking at the direction of their feet. This makes for spicy, fun reading no doubt, but its applications are skewed. These publications and several other viral content sites are responsible for people leaping to unfortunate and unwarranted conclusions.

There are far more effective ways to tell how a person is thinking or feeling than eyebrows, the direction of one's feet, and the color of one's eye.

Our internal instinct or gut feeling often resonates within us based on the clues and signals it picks up from other people. Sometimes, observing people in pain or discomfort triggers a sort of pain in our head, which helps us vicariously experience what the other person is experiencing. Learning to analyze people helps you come close to experiencing what they are experiencing; thereby helping you make better judgments and decisions.

At a more subtle and complex level, we are all designed to be social and empathetic. However, only a few of us possess the knack of reading people and connecting with them at a seamlessly automatic, and subconscious level. Specific parts of our brain automatically echo what the other person does or feels. For instance, have you noticed how someone you barely know smiles at you, your smile muscles activate almost involuntarily? On the contrary, when someone frowns, your frown muscles get activated too.

The human brain is automatically wired to pick up subtle clues that even our conscious mind may fail to register. For instance, when a person around is extremely angry and hides his feelings; we experience an almost instinctive feeling of discomfort around the person. He may not even look angry on the surface, but internally the body is reacting in the form of increased blood pressure or higher heartbeat rate. This is somehow picked up by our subconscious mind, which induces a sort of gut feeling that something about the person isn't right.

If you view it from the evolutionary perspective, plenty of our cognitive behavior can be traced back to resolutions gained from guessing what the other person is feeling or thinking. This is how we sought to solve most of our problems in the early evolutionary stages. We anticipated and guessed the other person's behavior in the absence of language only through their body language and expressions and based our own actions or reactions to it.

The sharpest trial attorneys have an inherent instinct for reading and analyzing people. They gather insights from everything from the nod of a judge to the way the juror glances at the accused to the way the opposing counsel speaks. They also go out of their way to train their clients in the art of keeping their verbal and non-verbal communication consistent with the image they intend to portray.

Clients are trained to give an impression of trustworthiness and innocence and eliminate any cues that indicate they are lying, which means minimal fidgeting, no darting eyes across the courtroom, and appearing interested in their case.

Learning to interpret people's verbal and non-verbal communication will help you view them in a less judgmental and more objective manner. For instance, when someone compliments you insincerely (alright, you aren't the one who falls prey to these tricks), it is easy to get swayed by the person's talk. However, when you learn to analyze people, you can tell the truth from deception and protect your interests.

Hop aboard then and get ready to read people like a pro.

Advantages of Being a People Reader

Why must you know how to read or analyze people you ask? Well, there are tons of answers.

For starters, it saves you a lot of time, effort, energy, and emotions by dealing only with trustworthy and credible people. Can you imagine the heartache of having to kiss a thousand frogs before you find your prince? You'll learn to watch out for signs of qualities you seek in a potential mate and avoid wasting time on people who don't show any sign of alignment with your own personality or the traits you seek in your partner.

When you learn to read people like a pro, it's easy to understand their personality, attitude, values, and mood, before they can speak a single word.

It is easy to tell when people are being honest or truthful and when they are deceptive. This skill itself is useful everywhere from interviewing job applicants to choosing a date to know if you've been cheated by your spouse. Your partner or spouse will never be able to get away with cheating again.

Selecting a compatible dating partner by looking for qualities, values, personality traits, and an attitude like yours. Determine if a person is truly interested in you, and then use that information to captivate their interest or impress them.

Boosting professional relationships and your career in general. When you understand what drives, motivates, inspires, and channelizes people; it is easier to connect with them to fulfill professional goals, derive greater job satisfaction, and maximize productivity.

You'll be amazed at how fast you may be promoted or get a raise with this invaluable ability to tap into people's emotions and channelize it optimally.

Boost your sales figures and multiply revenue by spending them only with clients who display favorable signs of purchasing from you. Knowing how to analyze a person will help you determine early signs of interest while interacting with prospective customers.

It will also help you negotiate better deals by pre-determining if a person is likely to agree to a higher price, thus raising your chances of acing negotiations. It helps you connect with absolute strangers, and makes you sway them in the desired direction. If you know that a person is reacting favorably when you mention a figure, you can quickly close the deal. Similarly, if they appear apprehensive, you can quickly restructure your figures to make more sense to them.

Learning to analyze people also helps you make a stellar first impression. It is easy to be popular, trusted, and credible in the first meeting when you know how to give the appropriate verbal and non-verbal clues.

Communicating with people is much more effective when you can read beyond their words. It gives you the power to interpret what's left unsaid. There is less scope for misunderstanding, conflicts, and drama. The communication is clearer, more effective, and easily understood as intended.

Tuning in to other's people's feelings and emotions allow you to be more empathetic towards them and reach out to them in times of distress, thus enhancing your interpersonal relationships. There is a greater opportunity to take control of the situation and avoid potential problems by doing things that are more favorable in the given circumstances.

Knowing how to read someone can be excellent for acing a job interview. You will know how the other person is talking to you and continue doing things they subtly validate or endorse. You will also quickly stop doing things that don't seem to impress them much. Bonus—you can impress the interviewer with your mind-reading skills (no, don't try it!)

As an interviewer or employer, it will save you the hassle, time, and money of hiring the wrong folks. You'll develop a trained eye for spotting honesty, integrity, and capability. You'll be able to tell when people are telling the truth and when they are resorting to deception simply to create a favorable impression. You'll also determine if they possess the traits needed for a role. Interviewers can easily pick the most capable, determined, and honest of the lot by applying people reading techniques.

Learning to analyze people's body language can make you an exceptional speaker. You'll realize when a person is truly interested in what you are saying (and keep the speech flowing in the same direction) or when you need to slightly adjust it to make it more appealing to the audience or when they are thoroughly bored listening to you (in which case a more dramatic action is needed to wake them up from their slumber).

Analyzing or reading your audience helps you gain information that can be built upon for establishing a common ground between them and you to make your speech even more relatable and persuasive.

For instance, if you are presenting a network marketing opportunity to people and their body language reveals that they are all ambitious people who love to lead a good life but who are thoroughly dissatisfied with their current jobs.

It is easy to influence, persuade, and inspire people when you know how to read their thoughts and feelings. It is also easier to establish your authority, credibility, and integrity as a leader when you know how to read people's reactions to your actions.

People will be able to elect the right leaders simply by observing their body language for clues related to deception, integrity, empathy, and power. By observing the person's verbal and non-verbal communication patterns, you'll be able to gauge if they'd indeed be the right leaders.

You can simply tell when they are bluffing simply to come to power, and when they are genuinely interested in the welfare of people or making things better for people.

Chapter 2. Introduction to Human Behavior Psychology

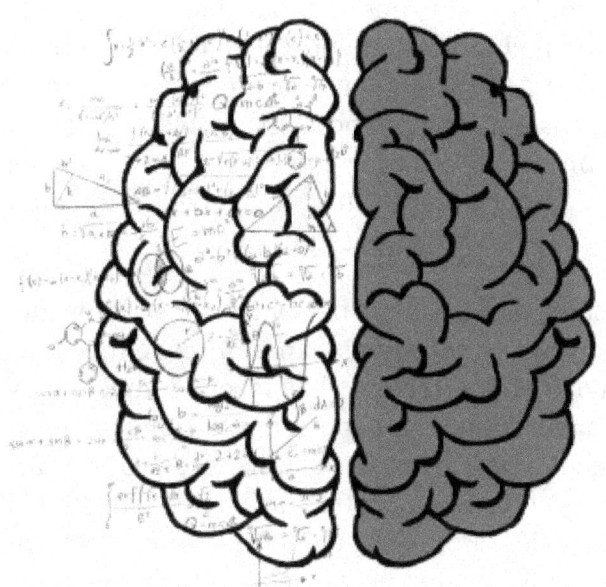

Human behavior is complex and dynamic, and this implies that the behavior of an individual depends on multiple factors, including the environment, genetics, instance, level of education, and age, among others. When human behavior is analyzed from a psychological perspective, human behavior entails the entire spectrum of emotional and physical behaviors that human beings participate in such as biological, social, and intellectual actions as well as how they are influenced by culture, attitudes, rapport, ethics, and genetics, among other factors. In this manner, human behavior is a complex interaction of emotion, actions, and cognition.

Relatedly, since actions capture everything that can be seen, then actions are a behavior component. For instance, actions can be captured via eyes or physiological sensors. An action refers to the transition from one state to another. These actions occur at different time instances such as muscular activation to sleep, sweat gland activity, or food consumption. Regarding cognition as behavior, cognition outlines mental images, and thoughts that one carries and can be both verbal and non-verbal. Verbal cognition may include statements such as "I have to wash my clothes," and, on the other hand, a non-verbal cognition may include the imagination of how the project will look after reworking on it. Therefore, the skills and knowledge by understanding how to deploy tools in a beneficial manner, such as vocalizing songs constitute cognitions.

Additionally, emotions are behavior and are considered as a comparatively short conscious experience defined by intense mental activity and a feeling that is not impacted by either knowledge or reasoning. As expected, emotions manifest from a positive to negative scoring scale. Enhanced arousal can trigger other aspects of physiology that are reflective of emotional processing, such as heightened respiration rate. As such, emotions can only be inferred indirectly, much like cognition via monitoring facial expressions and monitoring arousal, among others.

Psychological View of Behavior

The investment model concerns viewing human behavior in the form of work effort directed toward creating change. For instance, if Richard goes to watch a movie at the local theater, then the act of going to the movie is a form of investment. In this manner, the need to elicit the desired outcome motivates specific human behavior. If Richard gets to meet fellow fans and feels happy, then this can be regarded as the return of this investment. Akin to any other form of investment, human behavior occurs when one considers the cost-benefit-analysis of the desired outcome. For the case of Richard, he must consider time, calories, risks, and opportunity costs of going to watch the match at the local stadium.

It can be argued that the motivation to invest our actions in a specific behavior seems to emanate from evolutionary influences that make us prioritize food, sex, territory, food, and higher social status over other states of affairs. It also appears that behavioral traits, like temperaments and dispositions. For example, extroverted individuals find stimulating social situations more contending compared to introverted people. The learning history of a person influences the investment value system against this backdrop. An illustration of this concept is where an individual that liked the first season of TV series "Blind Spot" is likely that the individual is likely to be eager to see the second season of the TV series.

Another illustration of the human behavior investment model is where one is seated on the couch watching the news when an advert of a cookie activates in the person the desire to pour a glass of milk. The individual had a long day and is feeling worn out. In the mind of the individual, he or she calculates the cost-benefit-analysis of having to get up and pour oneself a glass of milk. In the end, the urge to go get a glass of milk from the fridge wins. However, a quick look in the refrigerator shows that no milk makes you take a glance at the dustbin where the person notices that the empty milk container. Then, the individual feels upset because his target goal has been interrupted and the person entertains the thought of walking to the store to get the milk, but the cost-benefit-analysis indicates that the person will spend significant time and effort to get the milk and so drops the idea. In the end, the individual settles on a glass of orange juice with mild feelings of annoyance.

As such, the investment model for understanding human behavior views behaviors in the form of work effort committed to realizing a particular outcome. The human behavior costs in the form of time and energy computed in the form of benefits and costs. Human behavior is largely a cost-benefit analysis according to the investment model of animal behavior. For instance, most animal documentaries on the behavior of animals can help you realize how inherently animals make the cost-benefit analysis. Take the case of wildebeests in African savanna plains that need to drink water and cross the river that is infested with hungry crocodiles. In this context, water and grass are scarce, and wildebeests desperately need water and grass. At the same time, the wildebeests must watch out for marauding crocodiles lurking under the surface of water ready to devour the wildebeests. Eventually, wildebeests must invoke an investment model of behavior to maximize the possibility of living, drinking water, and crossing the river to graze. Under this model, most wildebeests cautiously approach the river, ensuring that they near the riverbank when drinking water that would enable them to retract sporadically at the slightest hint of danger.

Correspondingly, human behavior is a form of commerce with the environment. Human beings actions are primed to maximize benefits from the environment. The mind is a critical component of behavior as it stores a history of what has desired outcomes as well as computing the cost-benefit analysis before one act. It can be argued that the investment model of behavior affirms the assumption that human behavior is conscious and well thought. Additionally, actions lead to lost opportunities, and one must pursue an action that best maximizes the intended outcomes. For example, if an animal spends time defending a territory, it will miss out on finding food.

The behavior of human beings can be considered from the understanding that human beings are social animals. Human behavior happens in the context of a social matrix. A social influence entails the actions that influence the investment of another person. For instance, when Richard was going to the movie, did he ask his girlfriend out or did the girlfriend ask him out? In most cases, social influence processes involve cooperation and whether the transactions move people closer or make them drift apart. Social influence also manifests as a resource. As a resource, social influence concerns the capacity to move other people in alignment with our interests. Social influence in this context refers to the levels of social and respect value other people show us and the degree to which they listen, care about our well-being, and are willing to sacrifice for us. For instance, if Richard is attracted to his girlfriend, and he agrees to go to the movie with her, then, this is an indicator of social influence as a resource. The girlfriend breaking up with Richard is a potent indication of a loss of social influence.

By the same measure, social influence is marked by the amount of attention from other people. In line with this understanding, the actions of a person will seek to attract attention from people or sustain the attention of people. Probably, you have colleagues or public figures that consistently act to attract and sustain admiration from other people. On a personal level, one is likely to act in a manner that invites admiration from colleagues, friends, and other people. The behavior and likely behavior of an individual is likely to optimize admiration from others.

Additionally, within the social influence model of human behavior, individuals are likely to act in a manner that invites more positive emotions than negative emotions from others. In a way, the need to attract more positive emotions from others is related to attracting admiration from others, but it is highly related to emotional intelligence. One can only enhance the likelihood of getting a positive emotional reaction from others if he or she has requisite emotional intelligence levels. Through emotional intelligence, one learns to show empathy and pay attention to how others are feeling. Against this backdrop, human behavior is likely to be reactive to how others are feeling, or it is likely to be highly considerate of others for the motivation of attracting positive emotions from them.

Equally important is the degree to which others will sacrifice their interests for the sake of another person as a mark of social influence. People with strong social influence will have tens to thousands of people willing to sacrifice their interests for the sake of the person. The behavior of the individual with great social influence is likely to consider that there are tens to thousands of people who are willing to forego their interests for the sake of the influential figure. On the other hand, the followers of the influential people are likely to take the actions of the individual as guidance or message of how one should act and live.

In most cases, human behavior requires justifications by legitimizing it. For instance, when you shout at someone, there are chances that one will qualify the behavior by stating that they were upset. In reaching justification, one assesses the behavior and the ideal outcome. For instance, the ideal outcome may have been attracting admiration from others, but one ended up embarrassing themselves in public. Expectedly, the individual will feel angry for not only failing to attain ideal reaction from the audience but also degrading the status quo. In this state, the individual will justify subsequent undesired behavior by drawing attention to the disappointment he or she got earlier on.

Using Richard and the movie example; Richard may have felt justified to make his girlfriend tag along to the movie and allow the girlfriend to show romance because of this what lovers do. The justification of his behavior and the girlfriend's behavior emanates from observation and learned patterns of what lovers do and not necessarily, of how each of them individually feels. Justification of behavior can be simply that is what others do, and so the individual is obliged to emulate the same. Try watching court proceedings for you to realize how people place significant value of justification for their behavior.

Relatedly at the organizational level, organizations have invested significantly in assessing human behavior during recruitment stages and as well as assessing workers. Human behavior is complex, and organizations seek the best bet in recruiting and retaining predictable workers. Most of the personality tests administered during hiring and appraisal processes are meant to help profile workers and have a predictable look at how each of the workers may behave. There have been attempts to determine a formula for human behavior as a simple system, but it has been satisfactorily concluded that human behavior is dynamic.

Chapter 3. Why to Analyze a Person?

The primary role of analyzing people is to establish the truth status of their words, actions, and body language. Verbal communication is likely to mislead where an individual indicates that he or she is fine when truly the person is feeling upset. The other critical role in analyzing a person is to attain effective parenting. Parents will attest that in most cases, what the child says, and what he or she is feeling may sharply contradict. Any person handling children will conclude that it is important to analyze the kids lest the person sits with a sick child, a depressed child, or a disturbed child thinking that the child is fine. In relationships, analyzing people is important to score their honesty about themselves and another entity.

In detail, we analyze people to gauge the level of respect they have for themselves and others. In most cases, we need to determine how much a person respects himself or herself as well as others. Relying on verbal communication cues alone will not reveal much about levels of self-respect one has, including the respect that the person has for other people. Fortunately, analyzing the body language will reveal convincingly the levels of self-respect and respect for others that an individual has. For instance, your dressing and personal grooming may indicate how much you value oneself. On the other hand, your facial expressions and posture will reveal much about how you regard other people, especially during a conversation.

Through the analysis of a person, we can predict their spending habits. Another major reason for studying people is to predict their spending manners. For instance, when looking for a partner, it is necessary to profile their likely spending patterns. Through analysis of their body language when luxury items and services are, mentioned, one can predict how the person is likely to spend his or her cash. Additionally, the analysis of body language can indicate any signs of addictions that the person has. For instance, through an analysis of body language, we can get mild hints of substance abuse, alcoholism, shopping addiction, or signs of obsessive-compulsive disorder. From this analysis of body language, one can predict the spending habits of a fiancée, kin, or employee with remarkable accuracy.

Additionally, the analysis of people helps understand their patience levels. Being patient is a desirable trait, and like most desirable traits; we are likely to force it to manifest to enhance our success chances. For instance, when looking for a date, the target person is expected to push the attributes of being patient when he or she is not. It is only through reading body language that we can make an early prediction of the levels of patience that the person has. As indicated earlier, the primary role of learning body language is because people tend to rehearse vocal communication, but it is a daunting task to uniformly rehearse tone of voice, the pitch of voice, gestures, postures, and eye contact to ensure consistency. Learning about the patience levels of an individual can help people around the target person relate better with him or her.

Again, the analysis of a person can reveal their hobby or how they spend their leisure time. In all social interactions, including workplace interactions; it is vital to determine the leisure preferences of the target person. A manager or supervisor in an organization will be interested in learning the actual leisure preferences of an employee with the understanding that during interviews people belt out answers that will enhance chances of being absorbed by the employer. Through analysis of the body language and incorporating verbal communication, it is possible to determine the leisure preferences of a candidate employee. In relationships, one needs to understand the partner wholesale, including their leisure preferences, to help create a middle ground with your individual leisure preferences.

Furthermore, a study of people can indicate their health status. As we will learn, our physiological condition influences the kind of emotions we express and how we express, including our physical behaviors. For instance, if feeling intense pain, then one is likely to frown, sigh, and sit in a non-upright position to cope or mask the pain. Similarly, if one is feeling dizzy, then he or she is likely to appear sleepy, disconnected, and frail. In healthcare settings, body language constitutes part of the diagnosis where the eye stare and movements of limbs are taken into consideration among other aspects of physical examination. Against this backdrop, analyzing a person can help reveal the underlying health status.

Equally important is that the assessment of people can help one determine their confidence levels. The level of confidence one has is important in determining how much the person will feel comfortable. In a team setting, the team leader will need to read the confidence levels of each member to determine how to delegate duties with each person feeling comfortable. If the confidence levels of an individual are low, then the individual is likely to be highly sensitive even to the mildest form of humor. In such a case, it will help to take into consideration the sensitivity of the target person when communicating informally. In personal relationships, it will help to help boost the confidence levels of the target individual while being sensitive when communicating and acting.

Another role of analyzing people is to determine their levels of composure. Even though it is akin to patience, but composure is the quality to remain restraint and calm even when a provoking message is being passed. It is one of the most desired quality but hard to manifest in individuals. Being composed does not imply that one mask or hides his/her true feelings, but rather, it is the quality of carefully processing negative emotions without letting emotions overwhelm you. When you comprehend the levels of composure of the target person, then you are likely to understand when to pause the communication or ease tension rather than guiding the target person to an explosion of emotions.

Finally, the analysis of people can improve their social experience. Overall, we are likely to analyze people to help us improve our social experience. We are likely to analyze potential friends to help us admit to only those people that best align with our wishes. Without analyzing people, we are likely to admit just any person as a friend and lose them shortly after that may make you think that you are the problem or that you are difficult. Additionally, studying people will help determine their true-life status and help you become more sensitive and understanding about their feelings, even their verbal communication speaks the contrary. At the household level, reading the body language of your partner will help you become more understanding and responsive to their needs.

The Advantages of Knowing How to Analyze People

So, why is it important to be able to analyze people accurately? It is something successful people naturally do anyway. They just ensure they hone these skills into something more refined, into strategies they can put into practical use in everyday settings. For when you are attempting to build harmonious relationships with others.

But first, it's a good idea to define exactly what analyzing others entails. What successfully reading somebody looks like. As we will see shortly, most of what we are reading within the other person is their body language (as opposed to the spoken words). Therefore, I focus more heavily on these principles. But, what exactly does body language analysis consist of?

It is essentially the study of everything which is being said outside of the spoken words, the intangibles so to speak. This will include everything in the non-verbal communication spectrum such as facial expressions, body posture, arm/hand/head gestures, handshakes, and any and every physical movement of the body large or small.

Then following on from the observation of these variables, the real benefit comes from interpreting and understanding what they mean, what the true underlying feelings, and intentions of the person really are. This is especially interesting when it comes to human interaction.

So, for the purpose of this book, the terms body language and non-verbal communication will be used to describe the same thing as they are largely interchangeable with one another. People will argue the exact figures with regards to the percentages of relevance in relation to verbal vs. non-verbal communication.

For instance, do you include eye movement (known as oculesics)? What about the depth and rhythm of breathing or the level of perspiration? As I mentioned above, I am personally including all these variables outside of the spoken words which also includes the tonality and intonation (paralinguistic) of the voice.

It has been suggested that all of this can equate to as much as 93% of the overall communication value, when this cannot be truly measured as it is entirely dependent on your own definition of body language itself.

Mehrabian who is currently a professor of psychology at UCLA is somewhat of a grandfather of modern body language study and non-verbal communication theory due to his work on the subject through the mid to late 1900s. The figures people most often quote come from two papers he published in 1967 which found that around:

- 7% of the message pertaining to the feelings and emotions of an interaction, come from the actual word(s) which are spoken.

- 38% comes from the paralinguistic element i.e. the way in which the words are said.

- 55% coming from facial expressions.

So regardless of your exact definition or interpretation of what body language entails, it is safe to say that it heavily influences any and every interaction. It is an agreed-upon fact that communication, in general, is anywhere between 50—90% non-verbal in nature with that figure climbing to the upper end of the range when it comes to more emotional discourse.

The types of interactions you might find yourself in with family members or critical business settings. In fact, any face-to-face or one-to-one meeting under any degree of pressure, including first impressions, will heavily involve a high amount of scrutiny and analysis of others. Whether you are aware of it or not.

So, remember that your non-verbal behavior will also be being observed during these interactions. However, it will be the person who has the greatest conscious control over their movements and gestures who will have the biggest advantage. So, make sure you heighten your awareness of these factors wherever possible.

Analyzing others, allows you to gauge so much more about a person and how they are likely to behave in the future. You will be able to much more readily decide if you would like to work with them going forward. So, pick up on these factors as much as you can, as they can have such a positive payoff on your decisions.

Chapter 4. Characteristics, Different Forms of Non-Verbal Communication

In addition to focusing on the words that someone is telling you, it is also important to look at some of the non-verbal cues they are sending out. These are going to include anything that the person does that adds to what they are saying. This could be things like hand movements, eye contact, facial expressions, how they stand, and more. It is pretty much any method that the other person is going to use to communicate, without having to use their words in the process.

If you genuinely want to analyze the other person, you need to have a good idea on how to read other people, and the non-verbal cues they send out. Most people are only able to portray so much when they are talking, but they can tell you so much more when you look at those non-verbal cues. Plus, how many times have you heard someone say something like "I'm fine," and then you see that they can't keep eye contact, or they look sad, and you know the words are false?

While the key to being successful in all of your relationships are going to rely on your ability to communicate and properly use words, it is not just going to be the words that you use that make up all of your communication. Your body language and other non-verbal cues are going to speak so much louder than the words.

When we are talking about non-verbal communication, we are going to look at some options like how much eye contact there is, the tone of voice, the posture of the other person, their hand gestures, and even the expressions that they have on their face. These are all powerful tools of communication that you can use to your advantage if you want.

These non-verbal cues can be useful to you as well. If you use them to your advantage, you can put the other person at ease, help to build up some more trust between the two of you, and even draw others into you like there is some connection, even if neither of you knows the other. However, if the non-verbal cues are not sent out the right way, or you choose certain non-verbal cues, it is possible that you are going to send out the wrong message as well.

By being able to improve the way that you use these non-verbal cues, and being able to read them properly, you will find that it is much easier to connect with others, figure out what they mean no matter what the words say, and can ensure that you build up relationships that are stronger and more rewarding than ever before. And all of this must come together if you hope ever to analyze the other person.

What is Body Language?

Before we decide to dive too much into this, we need to take a good look at body language, and what this means. Body language is going to be the use of expressions, mannerisms, and even physical behavior to communicate in a non-verbal manner. While you can control these a little bit if you think about them, most people are going to do these without even realizing what their bodies are giving away.

Whether you are aware of it or not, your body is always giving off and receiving wordless signals when you decide to interact with another person. All the non-verbal behaviors that you have will send out a strong message to the other person. These are messages that aren't going to stop just because you stopped talking either. Even when you are quiet and not saying a word; it is possible to speak in a non-verbal manner to the other person.

Chapter 5. Rules for Accurate Reading

As suggested, studying people is not reserved for psychiatrists but any other person even though psychiatrists are best positioned to analyze people. Analyzing people requires understanding their verbal and non-verbal cues. When studying people, you should try to remain objective and open to new information. Nearly each one of us has some form of personal biases and stereotypes that blocks our ability to understand another person correctly. When reading an individual, it is crucial to reconcile that information against the profession and cultural demands on the target person. Some environments may force an individual to exhibit behavior that is not necessarily part of their real one. For instance, working as a call center agent may force one to sound composed and patient when in real life, the person acts the contrary.

Start by analyzing the body language cues of the target person you are trying to read. Body language provides the most authoritative emotional and physiological status of an individual. It is difficult to rehearse all forms of body language, and this makes body language critical in understanding a person. Verbal communication can be faked through rehearsal and experience, and this can give misleading stand. When examining body language, analyze the different types of body language as a set. For instance, analyze facial expressions, body posture, pitch, tonal variation, touch, and eye contact, as a related but different manifestation of communication and emotional status. For instance, when tired, one is likely to stretch their arms and rest them on the left and right tops of adjacent chairs, sit in a slumped position, stare at the ceiling, and drop their heads. Analyzing only one aspect of body language can mislead one to come up with a conclusion correctly.

Additionally, it would be best if you lent attention to appearance. The first impression counts, but it can also be misleading. In formal contexts, the appearance of an individual is critical to communicate the professionalism of the person and the organizational state of the mind of that individual. For example, an individual with an unbuttoned shirt indicates he hurried or is casual with the audience and the message. Wearing formal attire that is buttoned and tucked in suggests prior preparation and seriousness that the person lends to the occasion. Having unkempt hair may indicate a rebellious mind, and this might be common among African professors in Africa, for instance. In most settings, having unkempt hair suggests that one lacks the discipline to prepare for the formal context or the person is overworked and is busy. Lack of expected grooming may indicate an individual battling with life challenges or feeling uncared for.

It is also important that one should take note of the posture of the person. Posture communicates a lot about the involvement of an individual in a conversation. Having an upright posture suggests eagerness and active participation in what is being communicated. If one cups their face in the arms and lets the face rest on both thighs, then it suggests that one is feeling exhausted or has deviated from the conversation completely. Having crossed arms suggests defensiveness or deep thought. One sitting in a slumped position suggests that he/she is tired and not participating in the ongoing conversation. Leaning on the wall or any object suggests casualness that the person is lending to an ongoing conversation. If at home, sitting with crossed legs suggests that one is completely relaxed. However, the same posture at the workplace suggests that one is feeling tensed and at the same time concentrating.

Furthermore, observe the physical movements in terms of distance and gestures. The distance between you and the target individual is communicating communicates about the level of respect and assurance that the individual perceives. A social distance is the safest bet when communicating, and it suggests high levels of professionalism or respect between the participants. Human beings tend to be territorial as exhibited by the manner that they guard their distance. Any invasion of the personal distance will make the individual defensive and unease with the interaction.

For this reason, when an individual shows discomfort when the distance between communicators is regarded as social or public, then the individual may have other issues bothering him or her. Social and public distances should make one feel fully comfortable. Allowing a person close enough or into the personal distance suggests that the individual feels secure and familiar with the other person. Through reading, the distance between the communicators will give a hint on the respect, security, and familiarity between the individuals as well the likely profession of the individuals.

Correspondingly, then try to read facial expressions as deep frown lines indicate worry or over-thinking. Facial expressions are among the visible and critical forms of body language and tell more about the true emotional status of an individual. For instance, twitching the mouth suggests that an individual is not listening and is showing disdain to the speaker. A frozen face indicates that the person is shell-shocked, and this can happen when making a presentation of health and diseases or when releasing the results of an examination. A smiling face with the smile not being prolonged communicates that one is happy and following the conversation. A prolonged smile suggests sarcasm. If one continually licks, the lips may indicate that one is lying or that one is feeling disconnected from the conversation.

Relatedly, try to create a baseline for what merits as normal behavior. As you will discover, people have distinct mannerisms that may be misleading to analyze them as part of the communication process. For instance, some individuals will start a conversation by looking down or at the wall before turning to the audience. Mildly, mannerisms are like a ritual that one must activate before they make a delivery. Additionally, each person uniquely expresses the possible spectra of body language. By establishing a baseline of what is normal behavior, one gets to identify, and analyze deviations from the standardized normal behavior accurately. Against this understanding, one will not erratically score a speaker that shuffles first if that is part of his behavior when speaking to an audience.

Furthermore, pay attention to inconsistencies between the established baseline that you have created and the individual's gestures and words. Once you have created a baseline, then examine for any deviations from this baseline. For instance, if one speaks in a high-pitched voice that is uncharacteristic of the individual, then the person may be feeling irritated. If one normally walks across the stage when speaking but the individual chooses to speak from a fixed position during the current speech, then the person is exhibiting a deviation that may suggest that the individual is having self-awareness or is feeling unease with the current audience. If an individual speaks fast, but usually the person speaks with a natural flow, then the person is in a hurry or has not prepared for the task.

Correspondingly, view gestures as clusters to elicit a meaning of what the person is communicating or trying to hide. When speaking a person, will express different gestures and dwelling on the current gesture may make you arrive at a misleading conclusion. Instead, one should view the gestures as clusters and interpret what they imply. For instance, if a speaker throws the hands randomly in the air, raises one of their feet, stamps the floor, and shakes his or her hands, then all of these could suggest a speaker that is feeling irked and disappointed by the audience or the message. As such, different aspects of body language should be interpreted as a unit rather than in isolation.

Then compare: For one to fully read the target person, try comparing the body language of the person against the entire group or audience. For instance, if one appears bored and other people appear bored, then you should conclude the tiredness of the person is largely due to the actions of the speaker for speaking longer than necessary. In other terms, the body language of the target person is not isolated. However, if you make a comparison, and it happens that the target person's body language deviated from the rest, then you should profile the actions of the individual accordingly. Making a comparison and contrast helps to arrive at a fair judgment of the target person.

By the same measure, try to make the individual react to your intentional communication. Another way of managing to read a person is to initiate communication and watch their reaction. For instance, establishing eye contact and evaluating the reciprocation of the target person can help tell more about their confidence and activeness in participating in the interaction. When an individual ignores your attempts to initiate communication; the person could be concentrating on other things, or the person feels insecure. Initiating communication is critical where it is difficult to profile a person, and one wants to convincingly read the person.

Go further and try to identify the strong voice. A strong voice suggests the confidence and authority of the speaker. If the speaker lacks a strong voice, then he or she is new to what is being presented or has stage fright. However, having a strong voice that is not natural suggests a spirited attempt to appear in charge and confident. A strong voice should be natural if the individual is feeling composed and confident in what he or she is talking about.

Relatedly, observe how the individual walks. When speaking to a target person, he or she will walk across the stage or make movements around the site where the conversation is happening. From the manner of walking, we can read a lot about the individual. Frequently walking up and down while speaking to an audience may indicate panic or spirited attempt to appear in control. Speaking while walking slowly across the stage from one end to the other end indicates that one is comfortable speaking to the audience. If a member of the audience poses a question, and one walks towards the individual, then it suggests interest in clarifying what the individual is asking.

It might be necessary to scout for personality cues. Fortunately, all people have identifiable personalities, but these can be difficult to read for a person not trained in a psychologist. However, through observation, one will get cues on the personality of the individual. For instance, an outgoing person is likely to show a warm smile and laugh at jokes. A socially warm person is likely to want to make personal connections when speaking, such as mentioning a person in the audience. Reserved individuals are likely to use fewer words in their communication and appear scared or frozen on stage when speaking.

Additionally, one should listen to intuition, as it is often valid. Gut feelings are often correct, and when reading a person, you should give credence to your gut feeling about the person. When reading a person and you get a feeling that the person is socially warm, you should entertain this profiling while analyzing the body language of the person. While considering gut feeling, you should classify it under subjective analysis, as it is not based on observable traits and behaviors but an inner feeling.

Expectedly, watch the eye contact. Creating eye contact suggests eagerness and confidence in engaging the audience. Avoiding eye contact suggests stage fright and shyness as well as lack confidence in what one is talking about. A sustained look is a stare, and it is intended to intimidate, or it may suggest absentmindedness of the individual. If one continuously blinks eyes while looking at a target person suggests a flirting behavior. An eye contact that gradually drops to the chest and thigh of the individual suggests a deviation of thoughts from the conversation.

Additionally, pay attention to touch. The way a person shakes hands speaks a lot about their confidence and formality. A firm handshake that is brief indicates confidence and professionalism. A weak handshake that is brief indicates that one is feeling unease. On the other hand, a prolonged handshake, whether weak or strong, suggests that the person is trying to flirt with you, especially if it is between opposite sexes. Touching someone on the head may suggest rudeness and should be avoided.

Finally, listen to the tone of voice and laughter. Laughing may suggest happiness or sarcasm. Americans are good at manifesting sarcastic laughter, and it is attained by varying the tones of the laughter. The tone of the voice tells if the person is feeling confident and authoritative or not. Overall, a tonal variation implies that the individual is speaking naturally and convincingly. A flat tone indicates a lack of self-confidence and unfamiliarity with the conversation or audience and should be avoided.

Chapter 6. Under Standing Body Language

While meeting people for the first time, we're all eager to make a killer first impression. There is an undisputed eagerness to say and do all the right things at the right time. Much as you'd like to believe that everything you say is making an impression on you, what you are leaving unsaid also says a lot about you.

Non-verbal communication (including body language, gestures, and tone of one's voice) plays an equally important role when it comes to rebranding yourself or wowing people. You can say everything you want to verbally but still not leave the desired impression because your body language is not making a wow impression or isn't compatible with what you are verbally expressing.

Even people who aren't trained to read people through body language can subconsciously latch on to signals that your non-verbal communication or body language gives.

Here are some tips for creating the perfect impression of body language:

- **Keep a Relaxed Posture:** Stand straight in a relaxed and easy position but don't lighten up so much that you look too casual or nervous. The worst you can do is sport a slouching posture. Make sure to be mindful, purposeful, and conscious of your posture now and then. A hunched back is a sign of being nonchalant or nervous/unsure about a situation. When you keep your posture upright in a more relaxed manner, you not just look confident but also feel more confident subconsciously.

- **Firm Handshake:** A firm handshake is a sign of self-assuredness, confidence, and high self-esteem.

With a firm grip, you give the impression that you are totally in control of yourself and everything around you. You'll get added points for making direct eye contact and smiling while shaking hands with a person for the first time. It shows you are genuinely pleased to meet the person and are interested in what they have to say.

Be careful of keeping the handshake firm and not crushing his or her hand or you'll come across as increasingly aggressive, and he or she may subconsciously dislike you immediately. You want to come across as confident and in control not overbearing.

A weak, limp and listless handshake, on the other hand, can signify an uncertain, nervous, and inhibited personality. It reveals a timid persona and a lack of self-confidence.

Mirroring the Person's Actions

Man is wired since primitive times to show affiliation towards another human through mirroring his or her actions. It is so deeply embedded in the subconscious mind that we don't even realize it is happening.

Now that you know it, use this information to your advantage. When you mirror people's actions, they form a subconscious connection with you, and view you as "one of their kind." The result, they end up forming a favorable impression of you or liking you almost immediately.

The act of mirroring should be gradual and discreet, not obvious, or the person will think you are mimicking them, which will be counterproductive. If the person is leaning against the bar while speaking to you, you do the same slowly. If they raise their glass to take a sip of the drink, follow suit. If they move their weight from one leg to another, gradually attain the same posture.

Look at the way they are using their hands. What are the gestures they make frequently? What are the typical words and phrases used by them? Try to mirror their gestures, expressions, and words. Match the tone of the voice. What is the typical way they speak? Do they speak in a restrained, hush-hush tone? Or are they loud and enthusiastic while speaking? Observe all this and try to incorporate as much of their verbal and non-verbal patterns as possible without making it too obvious.

Body language experts suggest aligning your body with the body of the person you are communicating with. Position your body to face him or her directly. This reveals your interest in engaging with him or her or giving them your complete attention, which everyone appreciates.

If the person you want to make a favorable impression on is standing in a group, and it isn't possible to directly face him or her, don't try to cut people off or leave them out of the conversation.

Rather, pivot your attention strategically towards the person you want to impress by making frequent eye contact with him or her (even while addressing the group), and offering a friendly smile. Don't stop a conversation and move your body towards him or her when in a group. It will only make you look eager to impress and overbearing.

Keep Legs and Arms Uncrossed

This may not be important when you are communicating casually with a close friend or family members. However, it holds plenty of importance when you are communicating with someone for the first time and want to create a stellar first impression. Like we discussed earlier, it is a defensive position. People will view you as guarded, closed, and secretive. You are less likely to come across as a genuine, open, and honest person. Crossing arms and legs can also be a signal of disinterest (pray don't do it on a first date or that all-important client negotiation) or absolute boredom.

Proxemics

Use proxemics to your advantage by maintaining appropriate physical space between you and the person you want to impress. Proxemics is nothing but the study of physical space when it comes to non-verbal communication.

Psychologists and body language experts believe that the amount of physical space a person leaves while interacting with another person reveals a lot about the dynamics of their relationship or the equation between the two. When you are meeting a person for the first time and trying to make a favorable impression, do not try to invade their personal space.

Maintain a minimum distance of four feet between with him or her as a rule of the thumb until you get to know them better. You can demonstrate your interest by leaning slightly in the direction of the person but don't attempt to get too physically close to them too soon. Even if you aren't leaning ahead, ensure that you don't lean behind. Just maintain a steady, relaxed, and upright posture. Leaning back can signify a lack of interest or boredom.

Small Talk Does Big Magic

The verbal exchange plays a huge role in determining the impression you create on a person. Learn something about the person before you meet them or attempt to strike a conversation with them. Digging a little into their background on the social media will give you a good idea about their likes, dislikes, hobbies, professional, etc.

Does he or she volunteer at a community organization? Do they play golf? What are the things you have in common with this person? These are good starting points for making a meaningful and engaging conversation.

One of my favorite tips for making a favorable first impression on people through small talk is going through the entire newspaper or browsing the net for the day's most happening news stories. If nothing else works, you can start by making a conversation about world events. This will make you come across as an engaging and well-informed conversationalist.

Just ensure that you don't share your views or opinion on something controversial, religious, or political and you'll do fine. Stick to general, non-controversial topics such as new discoveries, path-breaking research, advancement in technology, weather, global economy, etc. Small talk indeed goes a long mile when it comes to making a favorable first impression.

Show Attentiveness and Courtesy

I'll let you in on a secret. One of the best ways to be instantly likable and desirable to people is to listen to them. And listening doesn't mean having your ear in their direction. It means giving them your undivided attention and acknowledging what they are saying.

You can offer plenty of verbal and non-verbal clues that you are keenly listening to the person in the form of nodding your head, verbally acknowledging what he or she is saying and paraphrasing their sentences to show you are closely listening to what they are saying.

Do not, I repeat, do not keep looking at your phone or pretend to be distracted. If you want to make a favorable impression on the person, give him or her undivided attention, demonstrate good manners, and be polite/courteous towards everyone around. Mirror the other person's actions naturally.

Chapter 7. Analysis of People through Words

The eyes may very well be the windows to a person's mind and soul, but their words reveal how they think, process information, or offer insights into their character. Words represent both thoughts and feelings. Listening to a person's words can reveal a lot about his or her inner thoughts and ideas. Specific words can indicate the behavioral traits of a person who said or wrote them. These are words clues that help you predict the person's characteristics almost accurately. Though you may not be able to read their entire personality through words, you get a good idea about the behavioral patterns and thought the process of a person.

Our brain is nothing short of a marvel. While thinking, we tend to use more nouns and verbs. On the other hand, when we try to express these thoughts in spoken or written form, we emphasize on adjectives and adverbs.

The basic structure of a sentence comprises a verb and subject such as "I ate." Any more words that are added to the subject (I) and verb (ate) can offer clues into the individual's behavioral characteristics. Any words added to a basic sentence help you make educated guesses about the person. For example, if a person says he or she walked briskly; it can indicate a sense of urgency. They may walk briskly or quickly, owing to their need to be on time for an appointment, which demonstrates a more conscientious mindset.

People may also walk quickly out of fear or when there is a threat. It can be a threat in a potentially dangerous neighborhood or bad weather. When someone uses the word quickly, watch out for more clues about why he or she has chosen to use that word. Here are some pointers to read people through their word clues:

I Worked Hard to Accomplish My Dreams

The word hard here suggests that the person loves to chase goals that are challenging to accomplish and doesn't like anything that comes easy. It can also be an indication that the goal he or she is referring to was particularly tough compared to the ones he or she achieved earlier. Using words such as "hard" also reflects a mindset that is ready to postpone gratification to accomplish his or her long-term goals. He or she most likely holds the view that dedication, perseverance, and hard work is the key to producing stellar results.

At times, people convey a lot through what they leave unsaid.

Let us try to understand this with an example.

You are a server at one of the plushiest fine dining restaurants in your city. It serves multi-course meals that are much sought after by patrons. You have a family over at the restaurant for a multi-course meal one evening, and warmly welcome them. As a server, you introduce them to each course and offer interesting trivia behind each of the preparations, keeping them enthralled. You are sure they've had a wonderful time and enjoyed their meal. When they've paid the check and are about to walk out, you ask them if they liked the food. The man says, "The soup was good!" You aren't pleased. Why? Did he say the soup was good right? What do you think is the reason for your disappointment?

The answer lies in focusing on what he left unsaid. When the man said the soup was nice; he indirectly implied that the rest of the food or other courses weren't as good as the soup or were average. They were nothing to talk about. This is precisely the reason why we sometimes get offended when someone looks surprised and says, "you are looking good today." What they leave unsaid is, you don't normally look this good every day. Thus, while people convey a lot through the words they use, they also communicate a lot through the words they leave unsaid.

I Made Up My Mind to Buy That Home

If a person says he or she has decided to do something or made up his or her mind to something often, they may have considered many options before arriving at a decision. It means the person may be more contemplative and take his or her time to weight his or her options before concluding. They deliberate upon their decisions and are more analytical by nature. There are very slim chances of him or her being a rash or impulsive decision-maker. These are more signs of an introvert than an extrovert personality.

However, don't be quick to jump to conclusions as soon as someone uses the word "decided." Look for a pattern and other clues that point to a more reflective, thinking, and introvert personality. A definitive personality assessment needs thorough psychological observation and assessment and making sweeping conclusions about people based on a few words will only land you in trouble.

Extroverts gather their energies from others and seek greater environmental stimulation. They tend to use the trial and error method rather than deliberating upon a decision. Introverts will rarely speak without thinking, while extroverts tend to be more spontaneous.

It helps if you know beforehand whether a person is an introvert or extrovert to mold your communication pattern according to their predominant personality. For instance, if you are a salesperson, knowing whether your prospective client is an introvert or extrovert will help you determine how he or she makes decisions. Introverts take time to mull over things and make up their mind. Similarly, if you are negotiating an important business deal; it is important to understand if the other person displays characteristics of an introvert or extrovert.

If you notice a predominantly introverted mindset, give them more time to think before they make a decision. Pushing them into making a quick decision may go against you (they will most likely respond in the negative if they aren't given enough time to consider their decision).

On the other hand, a person who shows signs of making quick decisions may be an extrovert. These people can be goaded into taking fast decisions and actions. They can be pressurized into making instant decisions because they are more comfortable doing things without thinking excessively about them. However, one of the most important considerations is that people rarely exhibit a completely introvert or extrovert personality. Most people are a combination of both. They like to be around other people but also value personal time and space.

Chapter 8. Detecting Lies and Deception

So, having gone through the various elements of body language analysis when it comes to analyzing people in general, it's now time to identify some of the specific signals which could, in fact, imply deception. Signals which are unintentionally or designed to throw you off track.

Whether people would like to admit it or not, this is really what a person is after when they are attempting to learn how to read the thoughts, feelings, and intentions of others. They want to know if the other person is telling the truth or not? They would like to avoid being taking advantage of wherever they can, which is why this advice is so popular.

Starting from the lower limbs, the legs, and feet. Then moving onto the arms and hands, before finishing with the all-important gestures of the facial features.

Warning Signs

Legs & Feet

As I have also previously stated, movements of the lower limbs can very often be unconscious motions as we tend to think much less about what we are doing with them. It would always be wise to watch out for fidgety feet. People can mask the emotions of the face but will often release this tension with the feet.

Watch out for excessive tapping or moving as it is the biggest sign of impatience, nervousness, and possibly even deception. If the head, face, and voice are saying one thing but the feet are saying another; give president to the latter.

Arms & Hands

In general, analysis of the hands with regards to reading intentions can get extremely interesting when they start to interact with other objects or body parts. This is usually done to cover up some momentary conflict or dissonance within the person's mind. A disconnect from what they are saying and what they are in fact thinking.

The first and most obvious sign of this is hand interaction with the nose. It is no secret that the face and nose can start to flush with blood when someone starts to feel anxious or nervous when not telling the truth. Touching or scratching the nose is often an unconscious act of trying to hide this change of color.

This can range from minor embellishment and fabrication to full-scale lying. The old children's fable of Pinocchio, the wooden boy whose nose grew every time he told a lie is very apt here, and shows that the nose has long been synonymous with not telling the truth. It's called the 'Pinocchio Principle' when taught to psychology students.

Similarly, to this, if somebody is pinching their nose whilst listening to others speaking, can also suggest the person is holding back information, or perhaps stalling on giving a response. This is especially true if they are also covering the mouth at the same time. Kids will do this overtly and unapologetically. They will cover their mouth with the palm of their hand to signify that they have a thought in their mind, but do not want to say it out loud. This seems to have developed into a more subtle and subconscious act in adults.

These deception signals are not confined to the nose either, they can equally be exhibited by touching and scratching of the ear/head/neck. Essentially what a person is doing is compensating for the internal irritation they are feeling regarding the lie they are telling with an outside physical gesture to mask it. The one caveat here is that these signals can also be triggered by common and genuine nervousness, especially if the person is not confident with public speaking for example.

Chapter 9. Genetic Information to Place People in Different Temperaments of the Personality

The study of personality is broad, varied, and evolving. Different schools of psychological study have come up with different theories about analyzing personality, including dispositional (or trait-based study), biological, social learning, and psychodynamic.

Personality refers to a person's unique characteristics related to feeling, thinking, and behavior. It emphasizes predominantly on two areas—understanding differences between people with regards to specific characteristics and the bringing together all characteristics to understand the person.

Let's look at some psychological personality types to help us gain a better understanding of people's baseline, which can then be used in combination with verbal and non-verbal cues to help us read them even more accurately.

Type A, B, C and D Personalities

The Type A and Type B personality theory was first introduced by cardiologist duo Ray Rosenman and Meyer Friedman in the 50's.

Type A was known to be at a greater risk of coronary heart diseases than Type B since the former are known to be short-tempered, highly competitive, sensitive, proactive, multitasking, impatient, and always in a hurry. Type A personality people demonstrate an ambitious, hard-working, status-conscious, and aggressive disposition. They are always anxious to accomplish, which in turn leads to higher stress.

Type B, on the other hand, is known to be reflective, even-tempered, innovative, less competitive, low on stress, and unaffected by time constraints. If you're a classic Type B personality, you are moderately ambitious, live now, and work more steadily. Type B folks are social, procrastinating, creative, easy-going, modest, mild-mannered, and lead a more stress-free, laid-back life.

Later theories (that evolved to encompass even more personality types) found it constricting to divide all people into a Type A or Type B personality. Some people displayed characteristics predominantly from Type A but also displayed Type B traits. Thus, it became obsolete to classify people into two personality groups, which is why more personality types evolved.

A typical Type C individual has a fastidious eye for detail and is focused. They are inherently curious and are constantly trying to figure out things. There is a strong tendency to put other's needs before yours and avoid being assertive or speaking up. Typically, Type C will never mention straight away if they like or dislike something. Over a period, this leads to resentment, stress, and depression. They take everything in life seriously, which makes them dependable workers. Possessing great analytic skills, and intelligence, they just need to develop some assertiveness and learn to relax a bit.

Type D people have a more negative perspective of life and thrive in pessimism. Even a tiny event is enough to mess up their entire day. They tend to be more socially withdrawn and suffer from a deep-seated fear of being rejected, even when they enjoy being with people. They are at a higher risk of suffering from mental ailments since these folks predominantly lean towards melancholy and pessimism.

There is a greater tendency to suppress emotions, making them more prone to anxiety and depression. They expect the worst in any situation and do not share the feelings or emotions with people easily owing to the fear of rejection.

Trait Theory

The trait theory is primarily concerned with establishing the fundamental traits that provide a meaningful or coherent description of an individual's personality. It is also concerned with measuring these traits.

How does one draw a conclusion about an individual's personality based on the trait theory? He attempts to answer questions related to his feelings, thoughts, actions, and attitude. With the help of a personality inventory and rating scale, the individual's personality is determined. It is a combination of his responses and observation by the assessor.

Trained psychologists who observe these individuals rate them on a bunch of questions such as, how would you rate the individual's self-confidence? How would you rate the given subject's emotional balance?

Individuals are rated on several traits such as integrity, perseverance, sociability, dominance, etc. which in turn offers an analysis of the individual's personality.

Psychoanalytical Theory

This theory is dramatically diverse from the trait theory. While trait theory mainly relies on analyzing people based on what they've stated about themselves, psychoanalytic theory is an in-depth analysis of unique individual personalities.

Since the motivation is essentially more unconscious or subconscious, the analysis is believed to be more accurate. In the psychoanalytical theory, an individual's verbalization and behavior are a disguised manifestation of his most underlying subconscious/unconscious mind emotions.

The theory was first put forth by Sigmund Freud, when he compared a person's mind to an iceberg, where the surface makes up for our conscious experience, while the bigger masses underwater level represent our unconscious (comprising impulses, most primitive instincts and deep passions that influence our actions and thoughts).

Freud's much referenced psychoanalytic personality theory proposes that all human behavior is the direct result of interactions between the id, ego, and superego. This specific structural theory of personality focuses on the role of our unconscious/subconscious mind in modeling our behavior, actions, and personality.

Through the method of free association (dreams, experiences, childhood memories), Freud discussed analyzing people's most underlying feelings and emotions that determine their present attitude, behavior, and words.

Thus, most behavior patterns and actions are traced back to the individual's early childhood experiences or memories that they aren't consciously aware of, but are still lingering in their unconscious mind.

For instance, if a person displays more aggressive tendencies, it can be attributed to violent or aggressive experiences faced during their early childhood. If there is too much of a need to be accepted or please people, it can be traced back to being rejected by family members or friends.

Psychoanalysis is still widely used for helping people with issues such as depression, anxiety, panic attacks, obsessive behavior, aggression, anger issues, and more.

Social Learning Theory

This theory proposes that people pick up personalities or behavior patterns based on their learning from the immediate environment, and as such variations in behavior are a direct result of the diverse conditions in which we learn while growing up. Certain behavior patterns or personality traits are picked up through direct experiences.

For instance, an individual behaving in a particular manner may have been rewarded for it earlier, and hence is simply repeating what he learned through his direct experiences. For instance, someone constantly throwing tantrums and big on drama may have learned through early direct experiences that doing this helps them receive plenty of attention, which then becomes a behavior pattern. However, responses can also gain without direct experiences.

Since the human mind utilizes complex, symbolic codes to retain information based on observations, but behavior can also be a result of observing other's actions and consequences. Much of our observations and experiences are vicarious and complex. Reinforcement may not be needed for picking up or imbibing certain personality traits.

Carl Jung's Classification

Noted psychologist Carl Jung classified an individual's behavior or personality, based on their sociability, as introverts and extroverts.

Introverts are predominantly shy, withdrawn, and reticent, talk less, and are not comfortable in social settings. They tend to be more fixated on their ideas and are known to be sensible. It isn't easy to get them out of their shell and develop a rapport with everyone.

Extroverts are gregarious, outgoing, talkative, generous, courageous, and friendly. They are the classic "people's persons" who live more for the present than worry about their future. Their disposition is happier go lucky and positive. Challenges do not shake them easily.

Later, psychologists added another type to Carl Jung's classic classification theory. They argued that only a handful of people display extreme introvert or extrovert tendencies. Most folks, in fact, possess qualities of both an introvert and an extrovert. These people are referred to as ambiverts.

Ernest Kretschmer's Classification

German Kretcschmer's classification theory attempted to connect an individual's physical characteristics with his personality, and certain mental ailments that they were most likely to suffer from.

He classified people into various types including Pyknic, Asthenic, Athletic, and Dysplastic. Pyknic types are folks who are short and round. They are said to display personality traits of an extrovert—known to be outgoing and gregarious.

The Asthenic types, on the other hand, are people who have a slim/slender appearance. They possess a predominantly an introverted personality. The Athletic folks are people who have strong, well-built, and robust bodies, who display more aggressive, energetic, and ambivert traits.

The Dysplastic type essentially displays a disproportionate body and is not a part of any of the three previously mentioned types. The disproportion is due to a hormonal imbalance, where a person's personality also reveals traces of imbalance.

Psychological Analysis of Personality

Briggs Myers Type Indicator

There are several personality tests that individuals can take to have a psychological analysis of their most predominant personality. One of the most popular ones is the Myers-Briggs Type Indicator. It is a comprehensive and more reflective self-report that offers an analysis of people's personalities based on the way they view the world and wield decisions.

The test was created by Katharine Cook Briggs and Isabel Briggs Myers (Katharine's daughter). It relies on the Carl Jung's typological theory where he proposed that there are four essential psychological functions experienced by humans—thinking, intuition, sensation, and feeling.

In every person, Jung stated, one of the four fundamental functions dominate over others. The MBTI focuses on naturally found differences between different types of people, with a fundamental assumption that every one of us possesses a clear preference in the manner through which we experience the world around us, and these differences, in turn, underline our needs, beliefs, values, interests, and motives.

According to this popular psychological personality test, there are about 16 varied types of personalities. The test consists of a bunch of questions, where the respondents' answers demonstrate their personality type. It also offers insights on how a personality is most suitable for success in different areas such as career, interpersonal relationships, etc.

Here are the 16 main personality types as defined by the Briggs-Myers Type Indicator:

1. INTJ: These folks are predominantly imaginative, creative, and strategic. They seem to have a ready plan for almost everything in life.

2. INTP: Innovative, analytical, logical, and curious; they rarely stop reasoning and questioning things. They are essentially inventive, intelligent, and creative.

3. ENTJ: These are your natural leaders. They are courageous, imaginative, unafraid of taking risks, bold, and extremely strong-willed. They rarely fail to find a way or in the absence of it, will create the way themselves.

4. ENTP: The quintessential debaters, who can never resist a challenge that stimulates their intelligence; these folks are smart, argumentative, quick-witted, and curious.

5. INFJ: There are the unflinching idealists of the Briggs-Myers personality test. They are tireless, inspiring, calm, and mystical. The kind who let their actions speak louder than words.

6. INFP: These are the compassionate, kind, considerate, poetic, altruistic people, who never step back from contributing to a worthy cause.

7. ENFJ: These are people magnets, the charismatic, persuasive, and inspiring leaders who can hold their audience spellbound.

8. ENFP: They are creative, innovative, free-spirited, sociable, and always cheerful. These folks enjoy forging strong social and emotional bonds with others and are often the proverbial "life of a party."

9. ISTJ: Their reliability and dependability can seldom be questioned when it comes to offering practical solutions. Fact-minded, high on integrity, and

analytical, the ISTJ personality types are accurate, patient, and responsible.

10. ISFJ: The ISFJ people are warm, devoted, protective, and forever ready to put their loved ones out of harm's way. They are kind, altruistic, enthusiastic, and generous. They possess well-evolved people and social skills.

11. ESTJ: They are known to be exceptionally good administrators with an unsurpassable ability to manage things, people, and situations.

12. ESFJ: Their caring and empathy quotient is above average, which tends to make them extremely popular and social. They are always ready to step in when people need help and make for exceptional sounding boards or counselors.

13. ISTP: These are the quintessential risk-takers, who don't shy away from wielding courageous and bold decisions. They are forever experimenting and trying to master varied skills.

14. ISFP: Flexible, adaptable, magnetic, charming, and artistic, they are always eager to explore new things and thrive of novel experiences.

15. ESTP: These are smart, enthusiastic, and perceptive people who live a life on the edge. They are intelligent and make for energetic conversationalists.

16. 16. ESFP: The ESFP personality type is enthusiastic, entertaining, spontaneous, and energetic. Few other personality types can motivate and encourage others as much as these folks do. They have the most powerful aesthetic sense.

The Briggs Myers test is widely used in professional settings for leadership development, career selection, screening potential employees, promoting workforce, and team building.

Of course, like most other theories, it has earned its share of criticism for not being conclusive enough or generating "soft" results that cannot be completely applied in a business setting. However, despite the criticism, the test still offers a reasonable reading of a person's personality and can be a good value addition when it comes to reading/analyzing people. It can be more conclusive when conducted in combination with other psychological analysis techniques.

Certain types of personalities are more suitable for specific situations than other types. Knowing where others or you fall on the rating scale makes it easier for you (as a decision-maker) to know where people are most likely to be comfortable.

For instance, knowing that someone has a more introvert type of personality will help you make the most of their preference of working in structured, tinier, quieter, and more organized settings. You'll quickly figure out that these people may not thrive while working in a team and are more likely to maximize productivity by working alone. Similarly, extroverts may flourish in huge, loud settings, surrounded by lots of people.

The Briggs Myers can offer a reasonably accurate (though not comprehensive) baseline for helping you analyze people using a bunch of other psychological and practical people reading techniques.

Chapter 10. Verbal Cues

While there are many things that a person can say with their body; there are many more things that they can say with their mouth. There's a seemingly limitless amount of languages out there, as each specific language has many subparts. Think of how many different accents there might be in just New York City. As we continue to develop and blend different cultures and languages, only more will develop. It's hard enough to keep up with what we already know, but there are ways to still pick up on others' meaning without having to memorize every word in the dictionary.

Just because a person says a certain word doesn't indicate that they're meaning what they say. How many times have you said you were "fine," when really, you wanted to explode with thoughts? We say what we don't mean all the time because it isn't always easy to put words to our thoughts and feelings. Many people take their frustration or sadness out on other people when they don't mean anything that they're saying.

Knowing why people say the things they do can be one of the trickiest codes to try and crack. You don't always have to know exactly what a person means, in order to understand what they're trying to say. You can pick up on what a person's intention is by listening to how they talk and mixing that with their body language. It's important to read someone's mood so you don't say the wrong thing or anything that could potentially change the direction of the conversation.

Next time you find something on TV that's in a different language than any you can speak, try watching without subtitles. You'll be surprised to see that you understand part of the storyline. Don't look at what they're saying, but how they're saying it. Is there pain in their eyes? Do they look happy or sad? Sometimes if you can't understand what a person is saying, maybe because the room is loud or they're speaking softly, try looking into their eyes. You might get a better sense of what they're saying than if you just watch the words their mouth is attempting to put together.

There are certain specific cues that someone can give when they're trying to direct a conversation. When you're trying to persuade someone, you might want to try and use different keywords to help you in leading the conversation. Some people get too hung up on the actual words someone is saying when they should just be trying to listen to the message they're getting across.

It can seem difficult to try to crack what someone else means, but it can be done. Think about your pets. You can tell if your dog is sad, sleepy, hungry, or in a playful mood, but you don't have actual conversations with them. Sometimes you can analyze what a person is saying best by figuring out the noises they're making rather than dissecting every word that they say.

Emphasis Cues

When trying to persuade someone, you're going to want to have a pretty good argument already prepared in order to build your case. You might want to include some emphasis cues when you're speaking. It can be hard to incorporate these phrases naturally, but it's good to practice so you can become a better persuader.

"This is important," "you need to know," "let me explain," are all phrases that grab the attention of the person that you're speaking too. You might start to notice others' emphasis cues better after reading this section as well. You should be listening, and using in your own speech, phrases that seem to put emphasis on an important part of a conversation.

Sometimes, these emphasis cues aren't even actual phrases. They might just be verbal indications that something is important, such as someone raising their voice when talking about an important part of their argument. They also might repeat the word several times or stop for a pause for the listener to take in what they just said. Emphasis cues are important to understand in order to get a better grasp of what might be important to an individual. If you listen to what they're putting emphasis on, you'll be able to also formulate your thoughts and arguments around the things that are important to them.

Organizational Cues

"First, second, third," "to summarize," "the topic is," are all phrases that could be considered organizational cues. These cues help a person indicate that they are trying to organize their thoughts, again, maybe putting emphasis on the things that are the most important.

Organizational cues are important for you to use in your arguments in persuasions, in order to get people on your side.

You want them to know that you're listening to what they have to say, and that they should be listening to you. You're trying to formulate a plan based on both your thoughts and opinions, and not just the words of one specific individual.

Organizational cues allow the speaker to put emphasis on what's important while also maintaining a clear thought and direct focus. Organizational cues might not be phrases either. It could just be someone clearing their throat, redirecting the conversation back to a previous topic, or stopping for everyone to collect their thoughts.

Watch Your Pitch

Pitch is an important key when trying to direct one's conversation in their favor. Pitch is the level of your voice, and the overall sound quality. Someone with a deep pitch might have a more soothing tone, while someone with a high-pitched voice might make their listeners more alert. Not everyone can help the natural pitch of their voice. There are some people that have extremely low voices that are hard to hear, and some people just have naturally shrill voices that seem as though they bother everyone around them!

While your natural pitch can't always be controlled, you can at least help direct that pitch towards a more productive tone in order to keep your listeners engaged with what you have to say. Many of us let our pitch become too high and whiny when we are in professional settings, trying to keep our dictation sharp. If you feel like your voice is becoming high and shrill, don't be afraid to stop, clear your throat, and start again. The people around you will likely be grateful that you're adjusting your tone for their listening pleasure.

Be careful not to let the end of your voice go up when speaking. Many people, especially when talking on a phone, tend to let the end of their words go up like they're asking a question.

This kind of speaking is also common among those that might be giving a speech. They'll say a phrase very clearly with dictation, but they'll also end the sentence in a high-pitched way as if they're asking a question. This is something that should be avoided in order to keep the attention of your listeners.

It's important to find your optimal pitch. Some people have very soft voices that can be hard to hear. If this is the case, it's important to practice speaking up when it's necessary. Someone that tends to speak loudly should try talking low as often as possible to help balance their pitch out. The greatest way to practice is alone, and if you record what you're saying. You don't want to deeply analyze the way you speak too much, but practicing always helps, especially for those that find difficulty in speaking their voice.

It's also important to have a confident pitch to let others know they should listen to you. Someone that's always talking timidly or like they're asking a question will let the others around them know that what they have to say isn't interesting. If you're so unsure of what you're saying, why should someone else listen to you? The best way to ensure others are paying attention is to make sure that you speak with confidence.

Listen to Others

Talking about yourself can elicit the same good feelings that money and food cause. People like talking about themselves more than they enjoy listening to other people talk about themselves for the most part. While it can seem selfish, it's true that most people would prefer to talk about themselves. This means that when conversing with other people, you should avoid talking about yourself too much.

You don't want to make the conversation completely about other people, but no one will pay attention if the only thing you talk about is yourself. Giving advice can also be helpful, but people generally don't engage as often with those that offer too much advice, especially when it isn't asked for.

Listening to other people can be challenging for some. They might find it difficult to not let their mind wander, especially if the other person is talking too much about themselves. Some people will find that they're usually forming their next thought while the other person is talking instead of listening to them. If you find your mind wandering when someone else is talking, redirect your thoughts back to their words. Don't just listen to what they're saying. Watch how they're saying it. Listen to their voice and look into their eyes. People will notice whether you're listening to them. Even if they aren't skilled in body language; they will still be able to at least sense that you might not be fully engaged as well.

Don't just put an emphasis on listening to others. Make the conversation about them as well. Ask questions about the person, attempting to get to know them better. You'll find that people usually like to answer questions about themselves. This is often a technique you'll see in many salespeople. They'll ask where you got your shirt, or if you've had a good day. This is to get the person thinking about themselves, and they'll usually end up opening a bit more to the salesperson as well.

People don't like to be corrected. While it can be hard to avoid sometimes, most people don't want to be interrupted to be told that they were wrong. Most people will respect you much more if you just let them talk rather than trying to prove them wrong. This is very important to remember, especially when trying to persuade and analyze others.

Talk about "we," not "you." If you're trying to make suggestions, maybe to a spouse or friend about an improvement in their lifestyle, use "we" instead. Don't say, "you should try waking up earlier on the weekends," say, "we should get up early on Sunday and go on a walk together!" People will respond much better to suggestions if you include yourself.

Apologizing

It can be hard to apologize, especially for those with high levels of pride, but it's important in gaining the respect of the people around you. If you apologize for being late rather than giving every explanation you can, most will respond much better to this than if you were to try to make yourself look better with excuses.

They also like to see humility, and that you maybe aren't afraid to express yourself. If you can open up with someone and just say, "I'm sorry I didn't respond to your text, I was just having a really bad day," they'll usually be very forgiving rather than if you would've just blown them off.

However, don't apologize too much. It can lead others to not trust you. Sometimes we have the urge to apologize for things that were out of our control to make ourselves look better. We'll say, "I'm sorry the movie was so bad!" after going out for a movie night, even though we had no control over the production. This is nice occasionally, and certainly shows humility and vulnerability to those around you. But too much of it can also make you seem untrustworthy to others.

If you must apologize after every little thing you say, why should anyone listen to you in the first place? Next time you feel the urge to apologize for something that was out of your control, try saying thank you instead. After having a long conversation with a friend, don't say, "Sorry you had to listen to me rant!" Instead, try something like, "Thank you for being such a great listener. I'm glad to have a friend like you!" People will generally respond much more positively to a thankful person than someone that always invalidates themselves. You'll find that you start to treat yourself much better if you stick to this method of apology as well.

The Power of Your Body

Our bodies have so much power and not just with how much we're able to lift or carry. Physical strength is important, but even the weakest of people can control a room with their body movements alone. At this point in the book, you should have a basic understanding of what a person's body language might mean.

We can't get into every specific detail of what someone's physical actions might be trying to convey, but the framework for how to analyze those movements is there. Once you understand how someone else might be using their body to persuade others; you can start to work on your own skills of persuasion.

There are many ways that someone can use their body to convince others to do what they want, but it won't always work on everyone. Some people respond to sexual persuasion while others are repulsed by the thought. Some people respond to a physical threat from those that seem stronger than them, but others might be ready for the fight.

There are plenty of ways that you can use your body to persuade others without being sexual or physically intimidating. Keeping your body open and visible is crucial in letting others know they can trust you. Try making sure to remove physical barriers that might keep you separated from the person you're talking to. Step around a chair or table that's blocking you from making a full connection with the person you're trying to talk to.

This also shows that you're confident and interested in speaking your mind while hearing what the other person has to say as well. When analyzing other people's movements, you can also figure out what things you can do yourself to be more confident. Study certain celebrities and see how they hold themselves in various scenarios. Everyone has their own movements, but mimicking others can still help you find your own footing when it comes to having a persuasive demeanor overall.

Chapter 11. Highest Quality "Tells"—Facial Expressions

These can prove to be very accurate signals when you know what you are looking for. However, there is a final layer of study when it comes to analyzing people. The most powerful of all.

If the gestures of the hands and arms were more subtle and under greater conscious control compared with the legs, and feet; the movements of the head, mouth, and eyes are even more so. During interactions between human beings, over 90% of their gaze is directed towards the other person's face, so any signs given off here, regardless of how minor can be significant.

People intuitively know that the gestures of the head and face are under the most conscious control and attempt to mask them as best they can, which only further builds on the significance when they are spotted. So, it's time to start paying very close attention.

Head

The head is a very significant part of the human anatomy for obvious reasons. It houses the most important organ in the body for cognition and nervous system control, therefore exhibits some very powerful defensive and self-protective movements. In general, the head will lead the rest of the body with its movements for the most part. It will be the driver for all other subsequent body languages.

It is also closely connected with the facial features and these signals are often given in conjunction with one another. The difficulty in spotting some of the smaller movements and gestures will be offset by the proximity of the features i.e. the head & face is a small enough surface area to pick up on even the slightest signals as they occur.

Due to the flexible and dynamic nature of the head via the connection with the musculature of the neck; it can elicit a wide range of oscillating and rotation motions/gestures. This will include simple agreement or disagreement nodding and shaking, all the way up to more lateral head tilting. This tilting action can have a few meanings depending on the angle and direction of the tilt, but again is reliant on the context of the situation in relation to the facial gestures which accompany it.

A slight and slow tilt to either side with an intuitive gaze is often viewed as a submissive signal. It indicates interest and curiosity in what the person is saying. It also suggests a level of trust as the person is exposing the throat and neck, which also makes them appear smaller and more vulnerable. However, a tilt of the head backward tends to suggest a feeling of suspicion, distrust, and uncertainty, especially if combined with congruent facial expressions exhibiting the same. It's a more defensive movement, a subconscious rocking back of the head to remove it from danger.

Other than these stated tilting expressions, considerations with regards to the head can be reasonably obvious, such as speed and range of motion i.e. faster and more pronounced movements signaling a greater conviction and intensity to one's thought (in agreement or disagreement). Conversely slower and smaller nodes and shakes will convey the opposite in the persons thinking.

One tip for whenever you are trying to appear calm and confident or even attempting to conceal something yourself, is to make sure your own head movement is minimal. Keep it in a still, upright position whilst speaking clearly. Truly confident people exhibit very little head movement in truth. My mentor would always look straight at you and speak with perfect posture and statue-like poise. It was somewhat memorizing, and it would ensure I was entirely focused on exactly what he was saying.

Mouth

The mouth is unquestionably an integral part of human communication, but not simply since in combination with the larynx (voice box) we can produce sound and modern-day speech. The mouth also gives off very important cues with regards to analyzing people, especially when the other person is not talking.

Speech and oration are thought to be great conveyors of the message, but it is also a great way to conceal what a person is thinking. The very act of talking will often overpower and mask any subconscious gestures the mouth will be making, when the person is listening for instance.

Like the considerations of the hands, the mouth has many moving parts and can display a whole host on gestures which signify a great range of meaning. Unlike the nose and ears, which are typically only brought into play by the hands when assessing body language, the mouth acts independently to a large degree, and therefore requires greater and more detailed analysis.

One of the most obvious considerations is that of the smile. When assessing somebody's sentiment when they are interacting with you, one of the biggest giveaways of insincerity is a false smile. A genuine smile will be performed in unison with the rest of the facial features. All facial muscles will contract including those of the cheekbones and most importantly those around the eyes.

If a person is smiling only with the mouth, you should immediately question what they are thinking. This faking of a smile may also be done by dropping the jaw or with a "twisted" type smile which is uneven on both sides. Both unnatural movements of the mouth also typically suggest the smile is forced, and therefore the person is potentially concealing true feeling.

Another signal which is worth mentioning is the act of biting the lip or grinding of the teeth. Both motions suggest an element of tension, frustration, or even suppression of emotion. They are general displays of unease and should always be given credence when noticed. In fact, I am always wary of a person who cannot control their mouth movement and keep it still when they are not talking.

This goes along the same lines as excessive tapping of the fingers or playing with a pen. As we will see later when discussing the deceptions signals, movement masks feelings. Everything from biting of the lip, excessive smoking, chewing of gum, and even talking is typically used to keep the mouth busy in order to prevent it from signaling frustration and deception tells.

So, while stating that the mouth acts independently as a body language signal compared to the nose and ears, there is one traditional exception. The biggest and most obvious way to tell if a person is apprehensive or even being deceptive is excessive touching of the mouth and specifically biting of the nails. I don't need to point out the significance of this to you, if the person is unable to keep two of the most consciously controlled and important body parts still i.e. the hands and mouth, at the same time, something is up.

Eyes

I have reserved the observations regarding the eyes till last when it comes to analyzing others. These thought patterns and emotional cue giveaways can be such an important factor and tool in this process. So much so that many body language experts prefer to leave the study of the eyes, with respect to analyzing others, to a separate discipline altogether known as oculesics.

Whilst I do believe the eyes deserve special and individual consideration due to their accuracy in discerning intention; I always include them as part of the overall process of reading a person in general.

Eyes are what we predominantly use to assess the world around us, but it works both ways. Not only do we use them to look outward into the world; it has long been stated that looking into the eyes of another person can tell you a great deal about their internal thoughts and feelings.

"The eyes are the windows to the soul." (William Shakespeare).

Eyes are simply mesmerizing by their very nature and play a large role when it comes to hypnosis techniques. Even making strong eye contact with a stranger on the street can feel like a significant event. However, with regards to reading and analyzing others, we are more concerned with eye movement more than anything. To say the direction in which the gaze changes in relation to the behavior of others and questioning of them.

The following observations are intended to help you with just that, to give you any idea of what people are really thinking regarding their eye movement. For the sake of these descriptions "left" and "right" side is in relation to the individual, and not the observer.

Looking Left or Right

So, in general, a person will predominantly look to one side when being asked a question. They will either look left or right when reflecting, recalling, or remembering information. The side in which they look relates to the side of the brain they are accessing for the most part. The right-hand side is largely concerned with creativity, emotions, and feeling, whilst the left-hand side deals with the facts, figures, and memory.

Now, this is broadly speaking of course, and there are other intricacies and nuances we will explore below. But in a general sense, assessing eye gaze and direction can be a very accurate indicator of someone's true thoughts and feelings. Overall if a person is looking to the right it indicates that they are creating something in their mind; they are tapping into the creative centers of the brain to fabricate, guess, and storytelling.

This obviously isn't an issue if you are asking them a question and they respond by looking right and saying something like "I'm not really sure, but I imagine it would be like this." They are genuinely being honest here by giving you an impression of how they think it would be, and not stating they know it for sure.

However, if they look right and say something like "I was in that situation last week and this is how it played out." This is more worrying as they are stating something like an affirmative, something they know to be true from an experience and memory. However, when responding they were accessing the creative/storytelling part of the brain whilst they did it. This is not to say they are lying, but it is a big red flag, nonetheless.

To really assess these observations more accurately, you need to pay attention to whether the person is also looking up or down whilst looking to one side. In relation to the above example, if the person is looking downwards and to the right, this would indicate they are accessing the creative areas within the brain, but more closely related to emotion. They may just be recounting the feelings they had regarding the situation they are being asked about, as opposed to fabricating the answer.

However, if they are looking upwards whilst also looking right, this is more sinister as this would indicate that they are fully accessing the imagination centers of the brain and heavily suggests that they are indeed fabricating whatever response they are making.

Conversely looking left when answering such a question would signify, they were genuinely accessing memory centers and are telling the truth. This is especially true if the person is looking upwards and to the left which indicates recollection from the memory and image centers of the brain, greatly implying truthfulness in what they are saying. Similarly looking downwards and to the left also indicates honesty as it's a cue for recounting self-talk and rationalization about a given situation or subject.

So, make sure you are paying very close attention to someone's eye movements the next time you are interacting or asking questions of them. These movements can be small and subtle but can give so much away in terms of the person's true thoughts and intentions.

I was fascinated with the study of oculesics during my final year a Stanford. I would analyze literally everyone I met. I certainly felt it gave me an advantage when heading into business life too. Feeling out the true intentions of prospective clients and employees can save you so much time and money in the long run.

General Eye Contact

The only other important observation to make with regards to the eyes and their movements is direct eye contact itself. I have already suggested how it can be a powerful and mesmerizing thing, and will also say a lot about someone's personality, especially when they are speaking or listening to you.

This will carry greater significance compared with moments of reflection, after being asked a question for example. When eye movement can vary due to factors such as recollecting or imagining information, which I have described above. However, when talking or listening, strong eye contact always indicates honesty and sincerity with the occasional instance of nervousness, where it can be discounted.

So, this concludes the considerations with regards to the analysis signals of the head and face. Certainly, do not ignore the other body parts we have already discussed as they certainly have merits. However, make sure you are always paying special attention to the gestures of the head and face, as they can have such significance when you do spot them.

Chapter 12. What Are They Really Saying?

People talk in two ways; with words (verbal communication) and without words (non-verbal communication). Sometimes these two won't match in meaning, and it leaves you wondering 'What are they really saying? The following scenarios will give you a clear idea of the people reading skills we lack nowadays.

What is Your Boss Really Saying?

Suppose your boss calls you at around five in the evening (an hour before you wind up for the day) and says, "You may have to stay late at work today." If you only heard what he or she said, what did the boss say? The boss said, "You MAY have to stay late at work today." The "MAY" in the verbal aspect of communication is what you would have heard your boss say. It is very natural for you to assume that this word 'MAY' means the option to stay is yours and you choose to leave because you have that dinner date with your girlfriend or boyfriend.

During the time of your appraisal, you are given a low score, which affects your increment and your bonus whereas many of your colleagues have done well. You don't know what went wrong and you ask a close friend among your colleagues and he says, "So many times the boss told you to stay and you left." And you respond, "But the boss gave me the choice by saying I may have to stay late."

Your smarter friend gives you a look that could kill and it strikes you then that you have not understood what the boss was really saying.

What is Your Child Really Saying?

It's a Monday morning and you are rushing to get your children ready for school while you yourself are getting ready to leave for work. It's a crazy Monday. Your younger child comes to you with his head down and says, "Ma, I don't want to go to school today." You have no time to even look at him and you simply react angrily and say, "Let's not go down that road. The last time you said this was when you wanted to miss the test. Go get ready for school."

You give the poor boy no chance as you rush from task to task to ensure everything is done and ready before leaving for work. He gets dressed and leaves for school and you leave for office. At around noon you get the call from the school asking to come down urgently because your son is sick, and you need to take him to the emergency room. You wished you listened to what your child was really saying in the morning which could have easily prevented this emergency.

What is Your Girlfriend Really Saying?

Valentine's Day is coming up and you ask your girlfriend what she wants. She says, "Oh, nothing really!" You say, "You're sure?" She replies, "Yes, I am sure." Both of you smile at each other and everything is hunky-dory and there is happiness all around. Then, Valentine Day comes, and you take your girlfriend to dinner.

Both of you order food and the food arrives and you begin to eat. She is smiling and seems happy. You are happy. Slowly, as dinner progresses, the environment begins to freeze, and you have no clue what is happening. She has clammed up and she's not saying anything. She's picking at her food while you, in your ignorantly blissful state, are chomping down the amazing dishes that are being served. You wonder why she is picking at this amazing food and why is she not talking anymore. Is she ill? So, you ask, "Are you alright?" She responds, "Yes."

Again, in ignorant bliss, you continue to eat and after the meal, thinking there is going to be something fabulous happening at either one of your places, you call for the cab. That is when your girlfriend says, "Call for two cabs. I am having a headache and I am going home."

You say, "What?" and she shows you the fire in her eyes. You back off in fear based on ignorance. The two cabs come and that is the last you see of your beautiful girlfriend. Now, you think, "What was she actually saying?"

What is Your Best Friend Really Saying?

Your best friend has been behaving very strangely in the last couple of weeks. She is usually quite gregarious and sociable and enjoys the company of people. She never says no to most invitations for outings and parties. However, in the last couple of weeks, she has been saying no to everything with some vague reason.

So, now you go to her and ask, "Is everything alright with you?" She says, "Yeah, yeah! All fine. I'm just taking a break from going out because of an upcoming exam." You listen to her words and it makes sense. So, you leave the issue. After about a week, she has been admitted for depression. And you wonder what she was really saying when she said, "Yeah, yeah! All fine!"

Words are only one aspect of really listening to people. To analyze people well, you must have the necessary skills to listen to what they are really saying and that is what is lacking in most people today. We live in such a hurried and hasty world that we don't find time to pause, to feel, to see things that are obscure and yet, visible if only we could put a bit of effort at it.

Listening to what people are really saying requires you to go beyond their words. A simple phrase, "Nice morning," can mean something very different depending on what the non-verbal cues that are coming from the talker and the ability to read these non-verbal cues are what many lack today.

Words—A Gateway to the Mind

"Language is to the mind more than light is to the eye." (William Gibson).

So, having discussed the notion that body language is typically the main and determining factor when it comes to successfully analyzing others; it would be beneficial to take a brief step back in the process. To begin with assessing the thing which most people can more easily relate too when attempting to read another person's personality, and that is the words they are speaking.

The spoken word is certainly not everything, as we will see later, a person can be saying one thing with their words, but quite another with their movements and gestures. But you must start somewhere. Of course, the person could clearly be lying, and again we will also describe strategies to detect this later. But for the most part, the way in which you can initially decipher what a person is feeling and thinking; will simply be down to the words and sentence structure they choose to use.

Although the brain is an incredibly complex piece of cognitive machinery, when it comes to thought, we think much more rudimentary than most people would believe. To begin with anyway. Most people aren't aware of this, but the thoughts which arise in their mind initially only come in the form of verbs and nouns i.e. the words used to describe an action and the base context for it.

For example, "He jumped" consisting of "He" the pronoun which illustrates the subject and "Jumped" the verb which describes the action. It's not until we translate these thoughts into spoken word or written language; we add the adjectives and adverbs to really describe what we are thinking.

Anything added to this base sentence structure will modify (amplify/de amplify) the quality of the subject and describing words. This is where you can really begin to analyze people as the modifications, they choose to make to these sentence structures are voluntary. This will provide big clues into what is going on in the person's mind.

For instance, the phrase "He swiftly jumped" gives you an indication of the urgency of the action, but not yet a reason for this behavior. The person may have had to quickly jump as they tried to intercept a pass on the basketball court for example. A fearful person might swiftly jump at the sign of even the smallest animal or insect. Conversely, they may swiftly jump in front of oncoming traffic to save a dog from being hit.

People will include these adjectives to describe and modify a noun, in this case "swiftly" for countless different reasons. However, there will always be a specific reason for their choice. Again, it's here that you can start to interpret what they might be thinking.

So, with regards to putting these observations into practice, here are some examples to get yourself thinking along the lines of another person's thought patterns. I like these strategies as they are very unobtrusive in their implementation. There is very little probing or questioning needed. Just a simple observation of the words and sentence structure the other person is choosing to use.

I Persisted Until I Reached My Goal

The signifying word here is "persisted" which suggests the person values the importance of working hard. They strove particularly long with regards to this specific task, much more than they previously.

I Went Down the Right Path

The signifying word here is "right" which counter to the example above, conveys a sense of moral well-being and righteousness. The person is demonstrating that they have an accurate moral compass and can make the correct decisions when faced with important ones.

This is a beneficial behavioral trait for the most part and demonstrates maturity and a strength of character, in general. A person such as this should be praised for doing so.

I Sat Patiently Through the Meeting

The signifying word here is "patiently" which could imply several hypotheses about the persons thinking. The first implication is that of impatience, that the person gets bored rather easily which suggests a negative personality trait.

The second assumption is the opposite. Although the meeting wasn't of any importance to them, the individual sat through its entirety due to politeness and good manners. Regardless of which of these options may be true, it's clear the person is preoccupied with something else.

But, like everything I propose in this book, context will always be the defining factor when analyzing others. So, a definitive decision will be made after first considering the character and upbringing the person might have had, as well as the social setting you find yourself in.

I Decided to go on Holiday

The signifying word here is "decided" which suggests that the person contemplated their decision far in advance of their action. This may seem obvious with regards to a holiday, as much planning is required. But, this statement is also significant for my impulsive behaviors such as buying some new clothes or playing tennis for instance. It implies that the person is less likely to be impulsive in nature as they have thoroughly thought it through before acting.

It may also imply introversions, as introverts are thinkers by and large. They mull over decisions in their minds before doing anything. They prefer to sit alone and consult themselves on all manner of options whilst simultaneously recharging their batteries.

On the flip side of this are the extroverts. These people usually take the opposite approach to decision making. They take their energy from other people and the surroundings they find themselves. As a result, they make much more "off the cuff" and immediate actions in more of a trial and error type fashion.

You can see how much can be concluded from just the simple choice of words or the absence of them. These are just a few of the daily observations you can make with regards to the choices in vocabulary people will choose to make. They are designed to give you an idea of what you want to be watching out for when interacting with and analyzing others. So, ensure you are beginning to look out for these signifying words in your everyday interactions. You will start to pick up on so much more meaning with regards to what others are saying.

Chapter 13. How to Spot a Lie—Key Behavior That Indicates Deception?

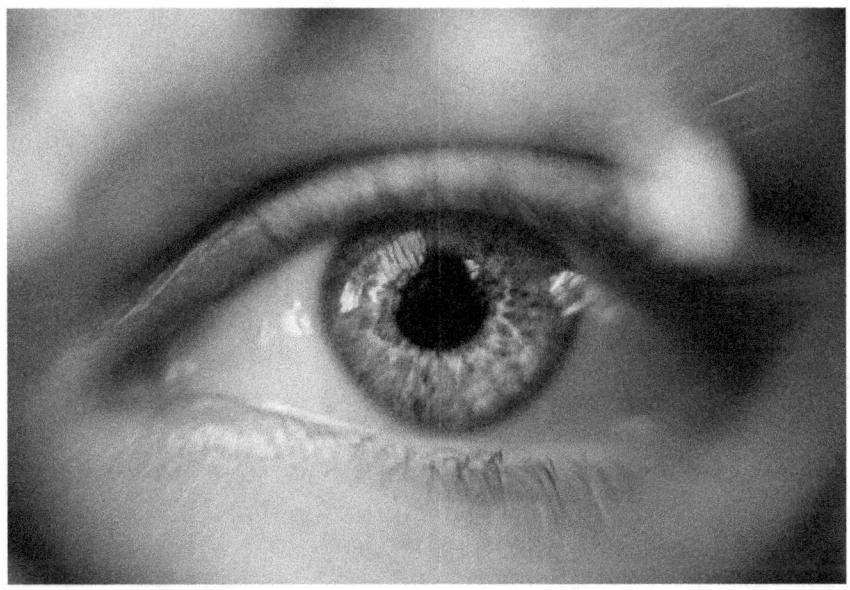

Detecting deceit will give you the rare opportunity to choose your associates wisely without having to say a word. The body goes into an immense ball of anxiety when a person lies. The trained eye will be able to detect these small variances that occur. Although words may speak their version of the truth, the body never lies. Deceit is the act of covering up the way you truly feel through seeking control. Oftentimes, that control is executed in a sloppy manner, thus leading to dominant cues that signal deceit. Whether it's a large lie or a little white lie, the results of dishonesty come with a variety of consequences. Essentially, people lie as a subconscious form of protection. They are either hiding their negative behavior or protecting their reputations. Even when used to exaggerate a story, they may be attempting to protect the fact that their life is truly boring. They want others to find them enjoyable. Thus, various lies are told.

One organization divides deceit into four categories of explanation and uses:

- **Anxiety**—seeking to hide the fact that they are nervous.

- **Control**—gestures or smiles that are forced or a grand attempt to stop the body from moving.

- **Distraction**—Frequent pausing or bodily actions in between answers is that person's attempt to distract you from their lie. By acting out these grand gestures, they believe they are making their stories believable.

- **Persuasion**—Deceit may stem from wanting someone to carry out an action that will result in the liar's favor.

Joseph Tecce, a researcher at Boston College, exposed the six reasons why individuals lie in addition to their respective character traits:

1. **Protective Lies:** This protects the reputation of the liar or even the victim from undue harm. They seek to keep their social status by not revealing true behavior.

2. **Heroic Liars:** These individuals will lie to uphold the greater good. For example, a popular episode of Sex and the City portrayed Carrie and her friend, Stanford, at a mixer. Stanford was interested in a handsome man across the room. He asked Carrie to go and find out if the man was gay or straight. She

approached him and let him know of Stanford's interest. The man looked at Stanford from across the room in utter repulsion. As Carrie went back to her hopeful friend; she told him that the handsome man was straight. She wanted to protect her friend's self-esteem by not revealing the truth.

3. **Playful Liars:** Playful liars accentuate their stories in order to provide a means of entertainment for listeners.

4. **Ego Liars:** Ego liars will cover mistakes in order to protect their reputations or status.

5. **Gainful Liars:** These are people who lie for personal gain.

6. **Malicious Liars:** These are the individuals who are out to seek revenge and harm others due to psychological challenges.

Many individuals are so crafty at lying; they have mastered the art of concealing their body movements. Sociopaths and psychopaths alike are so deranged; they feel no emotional connection to the lies. It is quite difficult to detect their inaccuracies because they are so connected to the lies. They may even begin to believe the lies. When considering the deceit of mentally stable individuals, however, there may be concrete reasons behind their excessive lying. Let's consider a few signs of a deceitful person and consider their traits.

The head can offer a slight indication of a person beginning to lie. When being asked a question, a liar tends to quickly move their head prior to responding. Interestingly, the face holds many of the truest signs of deception. We express honest emotions through the theory of timing. Researchers have found that, naturally, we hold our expressions between one and four seconds. When a person is lying or faking an emotion, the expression is usually held for a longer period. In addition, their symmetrical alignment can play a huge role in detecting insincerity. To tell if a person is being honest, notice the purest emotions are evenly distributed throughout the face. However, a liar will typically express their emotions on one side dominantly. Our speech and body movements should complement each other. So, if a person is telling you how beautiful you look while frowning and crossing their arms; it is safe to conclude that they aren't genuine.

Traditionally, the eyes have been closely associated with deceit. Previously, we spoke about the connection between dilation and interest. When we see something, we love or are attracted to, our eyes dilate. When in a relationship, a key indicator of a loss of interest rests in the pupils. When you ask your mate if your outfit looks great, they may say it looks awesome, but the pupils tell the truth. Excessive darting of the eyes or avoiding eye contact signifies some level of deceit. The person may be attempting to put on the demeanor of aggression, but they refuse to look at another's eyes. Are they truly as tough as they say they are? Interestingly, the right side of the brain controls auditory processing, big picture ideas, and decision making. When a person darts their eyes downward and towards the right; they are attempting to envision something, perhaps visiting a place they have never been. They may look down and to the right when thinking about what it's like to live there. When someone is lying, notice how they may repeat this same motion. Interestingly, they are attempting to envision something that didn't occur rather than recall a memory.

The body is also a clear indicator of deceit. You may notice the person's breathing patterns significantly speed up. Their chest could move faster, and their breathing becomes louder. Their shoulders and elbows are stiffly raised. This movement represents being caught, as seen depicted in cartoons. The robber may inadvertently stop in their tracks with their shoulders raised. They are trying to protect themselves by growing defensive. Psychics and spiritual healers utilize exposed palms to reveal the truth. Although controversial, many readers analyze the open palms to detect repressed emotions, predict future occurrences, and decode personality. When a person is lying, those palms of truth are suddenly closed and facing away from the subject. It's a subconscious way of not wanting to reveal their truth.

Although detecting liars is an essential tool to have, simply noticing a liar isn't productive. Effective communication in conjunction with understanding can help to reveal lies and reach solutions.

How to Spot Romantic Interest—Body Language Cues That Signal Attraction

Being able to detect if a person is truly into you can save a lot of time and heartache when dating. There are specific body movements that are unique to men and women that display attraction. Sure, words are powerful, but actions are groundbreaking. This form of body language is the most sensual in nature and inviting. Many of the common depictions on cartoons and illustrations are quite accurate when it comes to flirting. Women have a unique set of body language cues that are attractive to men. It complements their feminine role and can be used as a form of luring the man in. Men demonstrate a similar display of body cues that align with their masculinity. Oftentimes, the cues are so strong; they release certain hormones related to sexual attraction. The act of engaging in sexual pleasure is body language at its height. Since words are not commonly used as a sexual act, intercourse is the purest form of visually displaying that attraction. However, the journey from the first date to the bedroom is filled with subtle clues that could alter the destination. Let's consider the primary difference between men and women when it comes to displaying attraction.

Women

When a woman finds a male attractive; she may begin by locking eyes with him. She could give a subtle gaze and then look away. If this continues, the woman essentially wants the man to chase her. Simple touches to the body and even her curling her hair with fingers are used to flirt. This brings attention to the feminine qualities of a woman that may be attractive to the man. When a woman raises her eyebrows when talking with a man, they are signaling attraction. She may find the man to be physically handsome or admirable. Or, she may be so caught up in what he is saying that it moves her to agree. The lips also indicate attraction especially in the biting, licking, or caressing them. When a woman looks intently at a man's lips and then makes direct eye contact, this is a subconscious invitation to kiss.

When her legs are crossed inward, facing her date; it's a suggestive pose that indicates sexual interest. This is heightened when the genitals are exposed and involve a light caress. Women may also arch their backs to further elongate their spines. The curvature of their spine is a feminine quality that is attractive to the man. Slight exposure of the breast is a sign of intense flirtation. She is drawing the man into her womanhood to express interest.

Women may also "bat" their eyes up and down rapidly as a sign of flirtation. This brings attention to the lashes which, when elongated, are physically pleasing to the man. She may pair this with a slight giggle to signal attraction.

Oftentimes, women tend to "mirror" the movements of men. This signifies submission as the woman is showing respect for the position of the man. Inadvertently, she is following the lead of her date. Many sensual dances rely on the man leading and the woman following. Women subconsciously perform these acts to show respect for the men's masculinity.

Men

When a man moves his head slightly, raises his brows, and allows his nostrils to flare; he is indicating attraction. When paired with a smile, the level of attraction is heightened. Initially, a man will avoid making direct eye contact as he may be nervous or unaware of the woman's attraction level. In addition, men speak with their chests. If the chest is pointing towards the woman, he is giving her his full attention. If his chest is pointing elsewhere, he secretly wants to escape the situation.

Men want to appear dominant, masculine, and strong to perspective dates. They may stand with their feet wide and their hands on their hips in order to appear sturdy. If his hands are gracing his waistline, he essentially wants the woman to look near his genitals. This is a silent invitation to a possible sexual encounter. Men tend to show their attraction through their hands. Slight touches to the back, thigh, and arm indicate sexual attraction. However, a pat on the shoulder could be read as platonic.

There are universal signs of attraction carried out by both men and women. Smiling and a willingness to laugh without apprehension are valuable signs. Spatial awareness is a key indicator to reveal intention. When two people are attracted to each other; they tend to stand close. Their shoulders are raised and positioned inwardly which indicates interest. Even the positioning of the toes symbolizes attraction. As mentioned, the toes point to where they want to go. When the toes are facing each other, sometimes called "pigeon-toed," they are subtle signs of flirting. The man or woman wants to appear cute and coy. This vulnerable position subconsciously boosts sexual attraction. The palms traditionally reveal the truth. When a man or a woman is interested, their palms may rest in an exposed position. It promotes openness which indicates that the two would like to get to know each other.

The laws of attraction are traditional as they signify small psychological changes that are quite universal. When a person speaks their intent with body language cues to follow, you can guarantee their validity. By understanding these simple cues, you will be better equipped to make accurate perceptions about the intent of others.

How to Spot Insecurity—Small Signs That Show A Lack of Confidence

When people lack confidence, they display those characteristics boldly. Their posture and demeanor speak volumes so loud; others immediately respond. Unfortunately, these body positions prevent individuals from being treated with respect. They are more susceptible to being taken advantage of, passed up for opportunities, and even disrespected. Why is this the case?

Previously, we discussed different body movements that signal submission. While having a submissive personality is generally accepted as being mild, it doesn't equate a lack of confidence. Moreover, the body cues being demonstrated are similar in nature but intricately different. One of the primary indicators of a person lacking self-confidence is engaging in extremes. This can be found when individuals attempt to become "larger than life" by outward displays of dominance. Their initial appearance may seem intimidating, but their core is weak. They exude this fake confidence as a mask to cover up their inner conflict. Obnoxious, loud, domineering, and dismissive gestures are used to compensate for something they are lacking. Whether it's physical beauty, intelligence, or inner insecurities; your untrained eye may view them with admiration, even succumbing to their ploys. Once you are trained, it is obvious for you to see through their excessive demeanor.

Posture

A person's posture says a lot about their inward confidence. A tall, relaxed back indicates true confidence. There is nothing forced or excessively pronounced. When a person seems to loom over others with a widened stance; they are seeking authority. They may feel insecure about their current lot in life, so they attempt to make others feel small physically. In addition, slouched shoulders, a downturned chin, and legs close together are obvious signs of insecurity. The way a person positions himself in a chair also speaks volumes. If they are slouched, with arms tightly crossed, they are attempting to protect themselves. They may suffer from social anxiety and seek to disappear.

Eye Contact

When a person avoids making eye contact with someone by looking away or downward, they are secretly wishing to escape. They are fearful of what the other person is thinking, so they retreat to a safe space. You can always tell when someone is forcing eye contact as they blink less frequently to control the direction of their eyes. In summation, their gaze isn't natural. It appears forced and likely strange.

Touching the Self

To distract themselves from the current situation, insecure people will often fiddle with their teeth, touch their heads, or rub areas of their bodies. This is not an inviting or suggestive means to seduce. Rather, it's a coping mechanism used to calm the body and mind. Therefore, nail-biting is often associated with being nervous.

When individuals constantly fiddle with their clothing or readjust certain aspects of their appearance, they may feel insecure about their outward appearance. They may feel the need to fix themselves in order to fit the expectations of those around them. Oftentimes, people who try out new looks may constantly mess with their clothing because they are not accustomed to the style.

Excessive Movements

Leg, arm, and hand movements indicate nervousness or anxiety. When a person fidgets with different sections of the body, this is another sign of self-soothing. They are nervous about the conversation or even the environment they are in. You may notice that public speakers tend to fiddle with their ring or wrists when speaking about a challenging topic. In addition, placing your hands in your pockets, thus hiding them from the public is a sign of apprehension. You are sending the message of fear as you are attempting to conceal something.

As mentioned, the reverse is true for individuals who are immensely insecure. They attempt to overcompensate for what they are lacking by relying on superiority. Alfred Adler was a groundbreaking psychologist who studied human behavior. He thoroughly researched what he named the inferiority complex which addresses exaggerated behaviors to gain respect. Adler said people who feel inferior go about their days overcompensating through what he called "striving for superiority." According to the article, "The only way these inwardly uncertain people can feel happy is by making others decidedly unhappy." These individuals may use excessive physical displays of anger to gain control and ignite fear.

The slamming of doors, banging on desks, and even hanging up the phone with force are classic signals. When engaging in conversation, they rarely make eye contact perhaps busying themselves with other tasks. This outright dismissiveness is their way of showing others how important they think they are. On the inside, they may be recovering from past experiences of not being listened to. They may make others feel inferior to seek revenge.

Another sign of insecurity is excessive laughing. To fill the gap of conversation, a person may nervously laugh excessively. They are drastically uncomfortable and are at a loss for words. They may feel that laughing gives them the opportunity to make a fake connection. This could be accompanied by uncomfortable sweating or blushing. The body is physically revealing signs of embarrassment which increases our body temperature. Sweat may begin to lightly appear. The person may even begin to feel increasingly self-conscious about their sweat as well.

In this technology-filled world, cell phones are like extensions of the body. If a person constantly fiddles with their phone during social outings, they are probably suffering from extreme discomfort. They are attempting to calm their nerves through a cell phone screen. They may find scrolling through their social media as a form of comfort as it distracts them from engaging in a conversation.

Detecting insecurity isn't meant to give you power over vulnerable individuals. Rather, it is an inward ability to adjust your reactions to their behavior. If you encounter someone who is seeking to overcompensate by making others feel bad, you can detect that and handle them accordingly. You can see past their demeanor and ignore their "threats." When encountering a traditionally insecure person, you will know how to handle them with care. This knowledge will boost your ability to establish successful relationships and even boost social morale.

Chapter 14. How to Seduce with Your Body Language and Verbal Communication

This is not about fantastic pickup lines and being a guru at texting. You can effortlessly let a guy or girl that you like know with subtle signs that can be easily picked on the same way a TV receiver picks up signals from the broadcasting station. The dating game is changing, and body language is so powerful that it can make things easy for you.

One fact about seducing with your body language is that it is not always about what you are doing. You should also take into consideration the value of the actions. As a result of this, you must be well equipped in giving the right signals to your potential mate so that they can pick up on the subtle clues you are sending them. If you are giving the wrong signals, you will only end up scaring them away.

How to Seduce a Man with Your Body Language

You might be fed up of waiting for him to make the first move. Who says you can't make a move? Oh, I am not asking you to go talk to him. While that is bold, it also has some iota of desperation. You can send the right signals to announce your interest, willingness, and availability to a potential mate. In using your body language to seduce a man; you must know how to leverage on certain body positions to pass across your message.

Attract Him with Your Smile

You have a terrific smile. Use it to lighten up the mood and attract him. However, your smile must be genuine. A genuine smile involves the eye and the entire face rather than the type of smile that you must give because it's part of your job (like flight attendants and people welcoming you to a mall).

When your smile is genuine, the man will feel comfortable with you. He will know that he is welcomed to interact freely with you.

Touch Him Lightly

The idea is not to be all over him with your hands. Rather, touch him gently, such that it sends subtle signs that you want him. Consider these two scenarios: Juliet, while on a date, keeps rubbing George's chest, feeling the length and breadth of his goatee with her red fingers. Theresa, on the other hand, touches George's chin once or twice during the date. As the date proceeds; she brushes her knee against his thigh.

Both women are sure sending seductive signals that they want to ravage George on the bed. However, Theresa takes a calculated approach. While she wants him as much as Juliet does;

she has the self-control to communicate this with some restrictions.

Put Forward a Power Pose to Strike up Seduction

Think of super-humans. They appear in power poses with a confident look, and their hands are on their hips. Even if they are timid or shy, you cannot know as the pose conveys power and attraction.

Ladies can also employ this tactic by standing with their legs spread and shoulders straight. Your hands-on your lips will make you feel sexy and attractive in an irresistible way.

Lock Eyes and Lower Your Eyelids

In every form of human relationship, eye contact is very important and normal. In seducing men as well, eye contact is powerful. It is normal to look everyone you meet in the eye, even if it's for a moment.

However, when with someone you are attracted to, a deep, intense stare communicates many kinds of emotions, and some of them reflect sexual interest.

On making eye contact for a while, try bringing your eyes down and opening your lips slightly. This is a spicy move that allows him to know that there is chemistry between both of you. It tells the man that you are ready to submit to him sexually. This is the kind of expression quite a lot of women have before orgasm. This automatically makes him sexy.

Employ Your Lips

Your lip is a powerful attraction and seduction tool. It depends on you to use it the right way to communicate your interest. There are many things you can do with your lips.

Be sure to pick bold-colored lipstick as they get more attention. Red, for instance, is used to communicate passion. If you are not a fan of red, we recommend deep berry. However, be sure you are comfortable with whatever color you go with, and make sure it complements your clothing.

The next thing is how you use your lips. Men find a woman who bites the lower lip incredibly sexy and irresistible. Hence, once you lock eyes; try this many times, and couple it with a smile.

Play with Your Hair to Attract It

In addition to your lips; your hair is another terrific tool you can use to seduce a man. Be sure to use it wisely. Here is a trick you can apply: put the hair directly in front of him, then toss it back, and pull it over one of your shoulders.

All you need is one or two tactics, and make sure not to overdo it.

Use Your Face to Communicate Seduction

We make countless expressions with the face. Hence, the face can communicate better than the mouth. It expresses more than you can ever do with your mouth. Thus, your face can be a very powerful tool to reveal what's going on in your mind.

You can start by letting him know you are following the conversation by nodding while he talks. While he is talking as well, slightly tilt your head to reveal your neck. You are giving him your most vulnerable spot and subtly giving him a message of trust.

You can also employ the tactic of mirroring. Smile back at him if he smiles.

Lean in toward Him

You can communicate your interest through how close both of you are. Lean in toward him while he is talking. He will get the idea that you are engaged in him. As we have discussed earlier, leaning away is a negative body language that shows a lack of interest.

Just a few inches toward him is enough to send the message. His subconscious will catch the signals, making him receptive to the signal you are sending.

Wear What Will Make You Comfortable

On a final note, in trying to seduce a man, be sure to be comfortable with what you are putting on. If you are not comfortable with a bold-colored lipstick, then don't use it. The same rule applies to clothes. You must put on what you are comfortable with, and this does not necessarily mean tight and revealing clothing.

Guys do appreciate a little mystery in women's clothing because you leave his imagination all worked up, trying to imagine what it will be like under those clothes. Hence, you must put some creativity and a little touch of mystery in your attire. A little cleavage is fine. Show some skin if you are comfortable with it.

Be it a nice pair of jeans, a skirt, a T-shirt, whatever it is, your clothes should make you feel more confident. Also, remember that a tight-fitting dress will only make you uncomfortable, leaving you to adjust it throughout your date. I am sure you do not want that. Focus on what will make you confident. What do you think will appeal to your crush? Remember, a confident woman is damn sexy!

Final Thoughts on Seduction Tips for Women

In seducing your crush, you must know your tactic and what works best for you. Your friend might be great at seducing a man while watching the stars on a cold winter evening while that might not work for you. As we have emphasized, going with what you are confident with is the real deal.

Get your groove on and be sure to work with it. Bear in mind that your man will be attracted to a unique "you" and not some copycat gimmicks aimed at bedding him. Hence, be real with what works best for you for the best result.

Know whether you are interested in getting down to real business via sex or you just want to be noticed. Most of the tips that have been communicated here send the signals that you want to get in bed. Hence, know what you want before sending the signals. These are not the tips you use for a man you just met. You must be interested in committing.

Now, we move on to the gentlemen.

How to Seduce a Woman with Your Body Language

To the gentlemen, it is not compulsory that you talk to the lady before making your interest known. In fact, many guys have realized that no matter how good they are at talking to a lady; there are other pieces of the puzzle they just cannot seem to figure out.

It is not rocket science to understand how to harness the power of body language. Bear in mind that it is not that some guys lack the right body language. It is either you have been sending the wrong signal and the lady is picking on it and marking you as a no-go area or you do not know how to use your body language the right way.

That is not a call for concern, as I believe that is part of why you picked up this book. We will explore how to have cool, charming, confident, and charismatic body language to get even the most sophisticated woman.

Smooth Eye Contact

Eye contact is so important that you cannot rule it out. A poorly managed eye contact can work against your effort at getting the desired lady even when all else seems to be going your way. We are talking about fluid eye contact, not too much or poorly managed.

Not to worry, we have you covered. If you want a girl to relax and feel free around you, lock eyes for some minutes, smile for a moment, and look away. If she catches you staring, that is all right. The smile you gave already lightened things up. It is worth a shot.

Work on Your Posture

The way you carry your body matters a lot. It is enough to tell whether you are confident or not. Many guys have a bad posture, which could be a result of many things. If your job involves sitting too often, for instance, you will have a poor posture, which sends a message that you are not confident enough.

The worst part is that bad posture makes them close off. It makes it seem like they are not interested in a woman, and usually, women pick up these signals quite fast.

As a result, if you would like to attract a woman, you must pay attention to how you carry yourself. Walk straight and high without looking down and keep your shoulders at your back. This position might be awkward at first, but if it is the little price you must pay to appear confident, it is worth it I believe, as confidence is the new sexy!

Stand Tall and Bold

Just by looking at how someone stands and walks, we can deduce a lot. Therefore, you cannot leave this to chance. In addition to correcting your posture, as the previous tip pointed out; you must carry yourself with strength and confidence.

Here are some tips for standing bold:

- Let your feet and shoulders be wide apart. It will make you feel and appear big.

- Like the last point, keep your shoulders back. A simple way to do this is to see yourself as a hanger holding your shirt in the closet.

- As much as possible, keep your chin up.

- Let your arms be by your side, not behind you or in your pocket.

Combining all the above together will give you a killer posture that will make you unique. With this, attracting ladies will not be an issue as ladies love a confident man.

Play with Your Hands

Wherever you are, be sure to present yourself as approachable and open. You can have this by keeping your hands open, no matter how little. Making your hands open will keep you at ease, and you can get her attention without talking.

This is not about exposing your hands like a Buddhist monk—now that would be weird. The idea is to have some palm-open gestures as you are talking. This will keep ladies attracted to you naturally.

Avoid Fidgeting at All Cost

You do not want to give the impression that you are not in control and that you are anxious. Restlessness, fidgeting, and moving about will give a bad impression, one you do not want. Bear in mind that a calm, controlled man who makes a collected movement is a magnet to women.

Hence, slow down and take it easy. It shows focus and purpose. You will appear confident and sure of yourself as people will perceive you as comfortable in yourself and the environment. Besides, this will bring about some sort of mystery about you.

A word of caution, however, is that we are not asking you to move about like a snail. That would be very weird, won't it?

Deliberately Fix Yourself

Bear in mind that ladies notice everything about a man. No matter how insignificant you think it is, they do. You can employ this trick to attract that lady you are into.

Try to fix your clothing or adjust your tie around her. She will notice and catch the clue that you are into her as you are trying to appear attractive. This is a good one as it sends two sure signals:

- that you are interested in her, which is the main point

- that you care about your appearance

Hence, do not think twice before straightening your shirt before her.

Space Out

Humans these days, though evolved, are still controlled by some primitive social instincts. One of these instincts is taking up space. A lizard will urinate around a spot and defend this place fiercely against intruders. Okay, we are not going as far as being aggressive or talking about manspreading.

The idea is taking up a little space, some sort of territory where you can get comfortable, comfortable enough for that lady to notice you—that is the point that is extremely important.

So, when walking to the bar or wherever it is that you are, put your mobile phone and briefcase on the table and lean back on your seat. This sends a clear message of cooperation and confidence that women cannot resist. This is better than shrinking into a small space.

Be Mindful of How You Walk

It is a beautiful day, and a lady goes for a stroll. She notices this handsome guy with an expressionless face, hands in his pocket, and his head bowed. I bet the lady's impression would be that he is overwhelmed, stressed, or has something bugging him. All in all, the lady will mark him as a no-go area.

I hope you understand the importance of how you walk. You want your walking style to convey the meaning that you are approachable. This is about holding your shoulders high, sticking your chest out, and keeping your hands free, not in your pockets.

Chapter 15. Analyzing People via Their Verbal Statements

Everything that a person does or says reveals something about their personality. Actions, beliefs, and thoughts of people are aligned perfectly with each other in a way that they all reveal the same things concerning an individual. Just as it is said that all methods can lead to Rome, everything a person thinks or does can reveal a lot about their personality makeup and personality. The words that are spoken by a person, even if they appear to carry less weight, tell a great deal about a person's insecurities and desires.

No one doubts that the words we speak or write are a full expression of our inner personalities and thoughts. However, beyond the real content of a language, exclusive insights into the minds of the author are usually hidden in the text's style.

From our acts of dominance to truthfulness, we are revealing to others too much about us. You can quickly know the most important of all the people in the room by listening to the words that they use. Confident and high-status people use very few "I" words. The higher a person's status is in each situation, the less the "I" words they will use in their conversations.

Each time people feel confident; they tend to focus on the task that they have at hand, and not necessarily on them. "I" is also used less in the weeks that follow a given cultural upheaval. As age kicks on, we tend to use more positive emotional words and even make very fewer references to ourselves. A study has also shown it that the higher social class a person is the fewer emotional words he will need to use.

According to Pennebaker, style words include auxiliary verbs, prepositions, pronouns, articles, and conjunctions. He also goes ahead to explain the content words, which include regular verbs, nouns, and especially adverbs and adjectives. Here is the main difference between the style words and the content words. The content words are what someone is saying while the style words are how the words are said.

Women tend to use pronouns, social words, negations, as well as references to the psychological processes as compared to the male. This could be a surprise, but men tend to use more big numbers, prepositions, and articles than women. But despite all that, the way women speak implies that human beings are more open and self-aware of self-reflection. That is, according to Pennebaker, who also discovered that there are three main ways in which people speak when they are not saying the truth. He also discovered that the health of a person is likely to improve, not with the increased application of the emotion words such as joyful, happy, and sad, but with more use of the cognitive words such as understand, realize, and know. Public figures who have the tendency of addressing press briefings tend to use more first-person singular each time they are prone to committing suicide or troubled. When people tell the truth, they are likely to use the pronouns of the first person singular more often than other times. When the levels of testosterone increase in people, they will tend to drop in their use of references to other people that they are talking to.

Another study has also shown it that people who talk about traumatic circumstances or decodes to share some moments of feeling down or painful truth are physically healthier as opposed to those who kept the experiences secret.

Chapter 16. Signs of Confidence and Lack of Confidence

Signs of Confidence

One of the things that separate the weak from the strong is confidence. Confidence is an important characteristic that is vital for one's survival in this world. To forge ahead in life, stay ahead of the competition, and make your voice heard. Confidence is an important skill that you cannot do without. This explains why if a candidate goes for a job interview, no matter how smart, knowledgeable, experienced, and skilled they are, failure to show forth confidence during the interview will bring down the chances of getting a job. A confident candidate, even though not as brilliant and experienced, will easily outshine the other candidate.

In the same manner, your chances of getting your dream girl increase if you carry yourself with confidence rather than a gloomy and timid aura with low self-esteem.

Self-confidence is vital in every area of your life. There are signs to show that you have self-confidence. Hence, you can imbibe some of these tips to raise your confidence.

You Do Not Hesitate

In other words, confident people are assertive. They know what they want and how to get it. They are not dissuaded by ideas and opinions of others if they know they are on the right path. They are different from people who cannot decide, and they keep changing their minds without a clear-cut direction on what they are doing.

You Are Comfortable in Yourself

This is obvious. People who are confident do not seek to be like another person in a bid to appear cool or acceptable to others. They know their strengths and weaknesses and have come to terms with who they are.

They are confident in their ability to go after what they want and achieve it. They do not need to be approved by anyone or fake their personality for approval.

You Are Not Easily Influenced

How easy it is for people to influence and manipulate you is a big pointer to your level of confidence. Resisting influence is different from being proud. Rather, it is about being aware of who you are, what you want, and whose advice you take. It is taking responsibility for your life and being able to make the needed decision.

You Don't Need Approval from Others

Many people, in a bid to know whether they are right, seek the validation of others. This validation is important for them to feel good and know that their choices are right. Genuine confidence, on the other hand, does not need any validation since there is an inner witness that validates you.

As a result of this, you have peace with all your life choices and decisions, and you do not need anyone to make you feel good about them.

You Listen More than You Speak

Behind the mask of bragging is insecurity. A truly confident person does not see the need to brag. They are already at peace with themselves, their feelings, and their thoughts. They are after your thoughts.

As a result, they give people the freedom to express themselves. Since they are already at peace with their skills and knowledge; they seek to know more. Hence, they give others the opportunity to speak by listening more.

They Allow Others to Shine

No matter their input in any task, no matter if they did the bulk of the work, no matter if they were responsible for the success of others; they allow others to shine. Recognition does not really matter to confident people.

They are content enough in the success of their team and their effort. Hence, external validation, acknowledgment, or glory does not matter to them. Their satisfaction comes from within. As a result, they are neither afraid nor selfish to allow others to take the spotlight.

They Do Not Put Others Down

Behind the gossip, comparisons, and bringing others down is desperation to be like others and even to appear better than them. Truly confident people, on the other hand, always seek to be better than themselves. They strive to accomplish the ideal person they hope to be, not anyone else.

They Own Up to Their Mistakes

With confidence comes sincerity and honesty. Therefore, it is easy for confident people to let people know about their screw-ups. They don't mind being a caution for others to learn. A confident person sees nothing wrong in "looking bad" occasionally.

Signs of Lack of Confidence

Lack of confidence is something you cannot hide, and this will be reflected in many ways discussed below:

Inability to Accept Compliment

Someone with a healthy confidence level accepts compliments with a "thank you." They do not go about making excuses and giving a reason for why they do not merit it. They accept any positive reviews of themselves.

Such attention might make them uncomfortable, yet a major sign of confidence is being comfortable in accepting the praise from others. They might even see themselves as lucky rather than taking the glory for anything.

Lack of Eye Contact

It is usually quite difficult for people with a low confidence level to meet the gaze of others. The eyes, they say, are the window to the soul. People with a low level of confidence are worried that an eye-to-eye contact will make you see right through them, which will make you see their flaws. As a result, they are downright uncomfortable meeting the gaze of others.

Unnecessary Apologies

Apologizing when you have done nothing wrong is a classic sign of low confidence level. They will apologize for something they didn't do. When they hand over their project output to you, they will apologize for its quality even before you have had a chance to check it.

Their lack of confidence in themselves makes them accept a scolding, hence, in a bid to avoid it; they give preemptive self-criticism.

Being Indecisive

People with a low level of confidence will not be able to make simple decisions. Since they are plagued with self-doubt, simple decisions like what to say will be difficult. They have a fear of criticism since they know that making a wrong decision will warrant scolding.

In a bid to avoid this criticism or scolding, they pass on the opportunity to make any decision, or they turn the responsibility to others. They do not see themselves capable of making the right decision as the fear hinders them from weighing the pros and cons of their decision objectively. Hence, they believe it is better for others to make the decision and take the fall should something go wrong.

The Need to Explain

Someone without enough self-confidence will be compelled to explain their actions, whether right or not. No one is above mistakes, but people with low levels of confidence will feel the urge to give reasons for their actions. Even if they are successful, there is the urge to explain their choices and decisions.

Blaming Others

The inability to accept and own up for your mistakes is a classic sign of lack of confidence. In a bid to avoid taking the fall, they put the responsibility off themselves and pass it to the person they are complaining about. This is a classic sign of lack of confidence in that they do not see themselves strong enough to handle any heat that comes as a result of their mistake.

Making Excuses

Someone without enough confidence will be quick to make an excuse for any shortcomings and criticism. A confident person, on the other hand, will likely listen to the criticism and decide whether it is helpful or not rather than passing it off immediately with an excuse.

People who are quick to make excuses for their actions do so because of the fear of being a worthless person. Hence, they see the excuse as an escape route to manage and keep their ego intact.

Need for Acceptance

People with a low level of self-confidence do need the attention of others to feel good about themselves and their choices. They need the acceptance of others to feel worthy. Hence, the lack of this acceptance could be frustrating as it affects their confidence level.

A confident person, on the other hand, has realized that not everyone will approve of their choices. They know that all they need as validation is from within. This makes them good with their decision, whether others see sense in it or not.

Their Body Language Reveals It

Consider a person with a cheerful countenance walking with their head straight and their hands-free. Consider another person bent, with hands in the pockets. It is evident which of these two is confident. There are postures you take that reveal a lack of confidence. Hence, confidence is revealed by the way you carry yourself.

Chapter 17. Persuasion

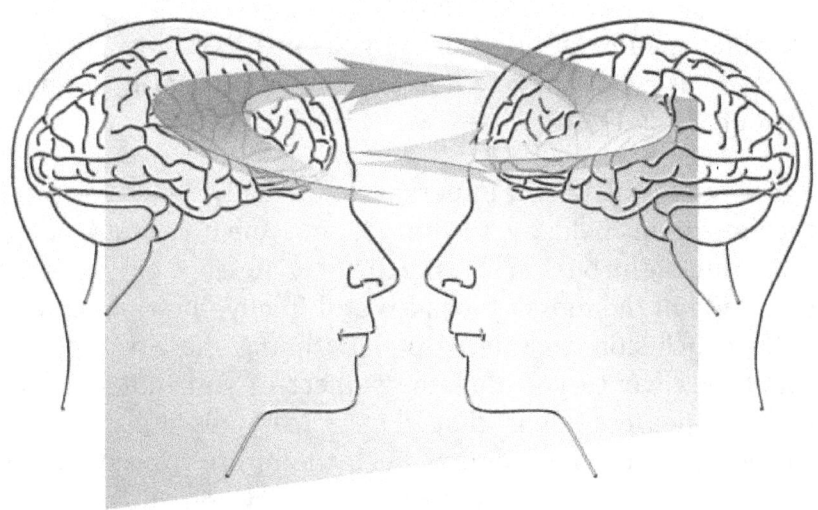

Persuasion is a deliberate effort to change or alter a person's opinions, beliefs, or attitudes toward an issue, situation, object, or person. This is usually achieved by transmission of a message which could be verbal or symbolic.

While persuasion could be used in a manipulative sense, it is in actual sense different from manipulation. This is because, when persuading a person, he/she is usually aware of your efforts at changing their point of view and willingly or reluctantly allows you to try. In this instance, the person listens and concentrates on what you are saying and then tries to rationalize your ideas with reality before then putting whatever conclusions they come to comparison with what they previously believed.

Your role in the entire dynamic is to state your reasons for the change you are prescribing, give illustrations, and evidence supporting your views and try to convince the target of your advances that your line of action or advice is their best bet. The main goal of this is getting them to switch to a state of reasoning or a product that you prefer. It is in this that persuasion resembles manipulation. Because your goal is still to push the target towards an outcome that they might ordinarily not have considered right.

The success attained in persuasion usually depends on the preconceptions held by the target and their strength, their perception of the person sharing the new message or idea, their perception of the message or idea and finally, their perception of the conclusion on offer. Upon outlining these reasons, it should be clear to you that the subject of your effort would probably possess ideas that are at least dissimilar, if not contradictory, to yours and as such the entire process would either hinge on your persuasion being very convincing or the ability of the target to meet a compromise between the conflicting ideas that would majorly mirror the changes you want.

Below are six major theories that strive to explain the way the human mind absorbs and reacts to information. Knowledge of these would greatly increase the odds of persuasion if you could pinpoint it in your target.

- **The attribution theory:** This concludes that people would either attribute actions and characters to people and objects respectively either in relation to the context they are being considered in or according to their own emotional disposition.

When they attribute using context as a guide, they are likely to come to decisions that take into consideration the environment of origin and situational factors. Such is seen when a person refrains from calling a product inferior or calling a person insensitive, instead of arguing that the product has been made from the best possible items available to the manufacturer and that the person is simply reacting as he has learnt from his childhood environment.

However, when considering their own emotional disposition, they tend to believe that whatever is convenient for them is the only right decision or approach for every other person. Consider this situation:

You meet a person at an event or gathering and try to start a conversation with them but instead of giving you a polite audience, the person appears preoccupied with their own thoughts or acts aloof. Angered or annoyed, you walk away and when asked for an opinion on the person; you characterize them as proud, arrogant, or self-important.

In this case, the characterization you have concluded is based solely on your emotional disposition and does not take into consideration, the situation or possible problems the other person might have. The idea is not to determine whether you are wrong or right but rather to analyze how you are likely to process information about people and things. You might be right about the person.

Another situation is when you have been accused of doing something wrong and you claim that your accusers have failed to see things from your own perspective and are only interested in their own point of view.

This is a perfect example of considering things as regards context. In this case, probably because the things said are negative, you'd notice the emphasis placed on contextual understanding of actions. There is also a slight hint of the dispositional thinking occurring simultaneously.

- **The conditioning theory:** In this case, the person is likely to do things if they are tailored and conditioned to look like their own decisions instead of as a result of coercion. This is most utilized in the advertising industry where commercials, advertisements, and billboards are used to convey information that would provoke positive feelings in the population of interest. They then connect such feelings to their products thus making you feel that the product would bring such a feeling into your life. Because of this, you are more likely to purchase their product, thinking all the while that your decision was an independent one.

This is usually possible because we generally perceive things based on our emotions and are more likely to buy things because they make us feel good.

- **The cognitive dissonance theory:** Based on this theory, it is assumed that people tend to aim for consistency in their thoughts, attitudes, and decisions. This is the reason why most people create principles that they strive to follow. Most people also seem intent on reconciling the contradictions as much as they can until they feel comfortable. I would give two examples of this.

Example 1

You have a very strong and deep-rooted need for canned food, either due to the laziness of having to cook meals or the frustrations at having to wait in queues for food. Then you are told that such canned meals could lead to cancer and you don't want to have cancer. But you also don't want to stop eating canned food. So, instead of stopping with the habit, you comfort yourself that millions of people like you have the same habit and would never have cancer.

The cancer theory might be untrue but your eagerness to dispute the fact or at least to make the consequences seem less severe is your own way of changing your mind or at least making the facts you have just learned seem less important or true. This is one of the ways of dealing with cognitive dissonance theory.

Example 2

Imagine a criminal with a conscience. This is probably hard to imagine but they do exist. In such a situation, his or her criminal tendencies are clashing with their tender hearts and causing a bit of discomfort. Such a person is very likely dealing with his/ her problems by giving in to the rationale that a criminal and wealthy life far outweighs the benefits of having a clean conscience or good heart.

Again, I am refraining from judging whether such a rationale is sound but am more focused on the fact that the person seems to give in to a rationale that overlaps with the general aim of most people to deal with his discomfort. This is another way of dealing with the cognitive dissonance.

- **The judgment theory:** This one is very simple to grasp. It simply proposes that when faced with a new piece of information or idea a person's reaction is dependent on the way he/she currently feels on the topic. What this means is that we're likely to accept something that resonates with our current belief, reject something that doesn't fit in with our beliefs, or stay indifferent to something never previously considered.

Therefore, when attempting to persuade a person; it is better to first determine their views on the topic to gauge whether you'd be successful and if your effort would eventually be worth it.

- **Inoculation theory:** The inoculation theory supports the view that even if previously uninterested in two points of view, once argued for, you are likely to pick the dominant point of view and stick with it. Here is an example of what I mean.

You have never watched a game of soccer in your life but one day you are relaxing on the beach and happen to find yourself stuck between two diehard soccer fans, who support rival teams. An argument begins about whose team is better and more dominant and they both turn to you, presenting their points like you are seasoned fan and after some time ask you to judge who's better. You obviously would pick the person with the better argument so as not to betray your own lack of knowledge on the subject. If in future another individual was to pose a question to you, inquiring as to which of those two teams is better; you'd probably find yourself arguing in favor of the choice you made then, maybe even with some of the same points that were used then.

This is the power of inoculations; the most powerful initial idea always takes root first.

- **Narrative persuasion theory:** From experience, I think we would all accept that stories have a more enhanced effect on perception and opinions than abstract advice. The attitudes and opinions of people towards objects and others tend to change when they are told compelling stories of such subjects.

The theory simply attempts to explain the heightened effect that can have on people if utilized properly. In this, the listener feels transported and this greatly affects their perception of events, making them more pronounced and vivid than they might have been if they had been expressed ordinarily and abstractly.

The Psychological Perspective

Ordinarily, persuading people would be difficult without the ability to properly organize and present an argument. But if inexperience in any or both of this is coupled with an inability to gauge and understand moods and stances, your task would be made many times more likely to fail.

The ability to instantly sense and recognize a person's stance on an issue is difficult, not to talk of performing the same trick on an audience. Because of this difficulty, most speakers who are attempting to introduce people to a new point of view always tend to ask questions that would enable them to gauge the stance of the audience before moving on with their presentation.

Immediately after asking such questions, they usually watch out for visible reactions from members of the audience, maybe a smile to indicate a previous knowledge of the topic, sitting up to indicate interest, turning away, or sighing to indicate disagreement or boredom or even a person willing to answer. These simple markers give you an idea as to how your message may be received and would help you map out a strategy of approach. It is also an effective tool as people tend to express themselves more sincerely when they do not feel particularly in the spotlight. So, if you are unsure, do not refrain from asking a few surface questions to test the waters or more aptly, to feel out the crowd.

It should also be noted that many people might give a negative reaction to one-on-one persuasion and would start arguments to further their points. The moment you realize that your attempt to persuade a person has deteriorated into an argument, it is advisable for you to walk away. Very few arguments occurring outside law courts ever get settled. Engaging in one would be fruitless and time-consuming. That time is better spent elsewhere.

Manipulation is similar to persuasion in that both aim to change opinions, attitudes, and actions from what they might have been to whatever you prefer and I had also stated that they differ from one another in that, persuasion is a more direct form of securing the change you desire, while manipulation requires you to operate in secret using emotional exploitation. Now, I would like to expatiate on the relationship between manipulation and persuasion or rather how persuasion can be adopted as a tool for manipulators.

This is not rocket science and needs only a simple alteration in approach to persuasion. It would require you to couple the ability to make compelling, irrefutable arguments with your ability to recognize emotional markers. Once both are in sync; you are ready to move. But why these two? The answer to that is rather simple. If you recognize an emotion to be dominant in the target and fell the need to convince, he or she to do something without outright manipulation, most likely due to the presence of friends and family, wouldn't it be better to play on such emotion and use it as a lever or platform with which you propel your point of view rather than just riding in without a strategy.

Therefore, persuasion makes manipulation look humane and might even reduce the noticeability of your ploy. It enables the manipulator, you, to touch on the emotions of a target for a reaction, but instead of making your telling moves under a shroud all the time; you adopt clever arguments and let them do the convincing for you. The trick, however, is to always get the emotion right.

Chapter 18. Conclusion

I sincerely hope it has offered you several valuable insights into reading people's personalities through proven strategies, tried, and tested subconscious techniques and a treasure trove of practical tips. These tips can be applied just anywhere, in any situation from business to interpersonal relationships to social settings to negotiations.

Whether you want to figure out the personality of a potentially big client during a negotiation or the characteristics of the hot new prospective date you have your eyes on, this book is a handy resource for helping you read others effectively. If there's a single largest skill that spells success in today's world, it is the ability to read people.

This allows you to mold your message according to the personality of the other person to accomplish optimally beneficial communication.

The next step is to use the book and apply it in your daily life in small, gradual ways to begin with. Start by observing people at the airport or doctor's clinic when you have some time at hand. The interest will quickly catch on, and you'll find yourself taking a deep interest in reading and analyzing people.

Our smiles are one of the most powerful tools we've been given. You can turn any situation from bad to good just by turning up the corners of your mouth. Some people feel as though if they don't have straight teeth or smiles that are bright white; they aren't worth anything. Even those that don't have all their teeth can have much more beautiful smiles than someone that's spent thousands on dental work.

A smile isn't just about what teeth you're showing. It's a way to engage another person. Studies have proven that most people will smile if someone else smiles at them first. If they do smile, they'll end up having a better mood overall. It can seem weird, but simply smiling can lift someone's spirits. Next time you are feeling particularly down, smile. It sounds so silly, but it might work. Smile repeatedly, and even though it might not turn your mood around, it will certainly help to at least temporarily lift your spirits.

However, for the times when you are in more relaxed and comfortable settings, always watch out for these subtle hand cues or "tells" when you suspect someone is trying to cover something up or be untruthful with what they are saying. This will obviously overlap heavily with eye movement and other facial expressions which we will move onto next.

Finally, along with watching out for fidgety feet; you also always need to do the same with arms and hands. Now it's a little less of a significant tell compared to the feet, as the hands are under greater conscious control. But once more, you need to watch out for excessive tapping of the fingers or scratching or the arms, neck, or face which can simply be an indication of impatience or nervousness, but possibly a sign of deception.

Facial Expressions

It is something that can be picked up upon quite naturally by most people as there will be a clear and distinct difference in the signals given-off by the eyes and mouth by and large. The mouth may be smiling, but the eyes will not be.

I have also described the implications the various eye movements will have on potentially deceitful statements made by people. So, make sure you go over the information in practice on everyone you come across. The only other truly significant and consistent "tell" you can rely on when it comes to deception detectors for the facial expressions; is blinking of the eyes.

Like every other body part, watch out for erratic behavior and excessive movement of the eyes. The eyes should blink between 5–15 times a minute, and anything over 20 times should be viewed as abnormal and suspicious (unless they obviously have some momentary irritation of course).

Manipulation

48 power techniques of persuasion of NLP to influence and control the mind and emotions of people, through hypnosis and effective methods of dark psychology, developing empathic skills

Chapter 1. Introduction

Emotional intelligence is thought to be among the fastest growing job skills, and for reasonable. People that have high emotional intelligence have an advantage over others at work mainly because they cope better under pressure, find it simpler to function in multicultural environments, and being good listeners, make emphatic colleagues and great leaders possibly.

Therefore, developing emotional intelligence makes it simpler to cope with the needs of a stressful and fast-paced life of the 21st century. That is particularly important for those that discover themselves in high-paid, prestigious, or leadership positions.

Therefore, the main benefit of having high emotional intelligence is normally that focusing on how to successfully manage emotions and having the ability to understand and cooperate with others easily, you stand to be a secured asset to whomever you work for.

Besides, intelligent people process their emotions before giving an answer to them emotionally. Quite simply, they believe before they speak. This might not seem very essential, but it's likely that if a habit is had by you of making ill-informed comments, you will ultimately come to regret them.

This is perhaps particularly relevant for the Western culture where people usually don't like silence and tend to answer questions or make comments without thinking. Or worse even, believe that every silence needs to be filled up with a witty comment or a remark.

Words can both help and hurt, and your choice of words says a total lot about you. So, a great way of raising your emotional intelligence is to become more aware of the implications of everything you are saying.

Chapter 2. The Foundations of Manipulation

Now, while all of us will try to manipulate another person on occasion to help us get things done or to get something else we want, not everyone is easily manipulated. Sure, you could probably get someone to give you a ride on occasion, but that does not mean that you would be able to do some of the emotional and covert manipulative techniques that we talked about on them. There are some types of people who are more susceptible to being manipulated, who make the job of the manipulator easier, and these people will often find that they are not pulling the strings at all in their own lives.

So, how do you know if you are a prime target for a manipulator? Could you be one of those people who manipulators are looking for all the time? Some of the people who can be easily manipulated include:

- **Those who rely on others for information**: If you rely on someone else for information, you are just asking for someone to try and fool you. You must be alert to the things that are going on around you, and you must learn to make informed decisions that use common sense. Otherwise, a manipulator will quickly take over, and you will just go along with them because it is the easiest path.

- **Those who do not think through their decisions**: For those who like to think quickly, a manipulator is helpful to them. The manipulator can come in and help them make the decision. Someone who thinks through their decisions will not like the idea of someone else coming in and trying to do the work for them. But those who want to get the decision-making over with quickly will appreciate the help that the manipulator will give.

- **Those who have low self-confidence**: Those who have low self-confidence are perfect targets. These individuals often are overlooked by others and may not have a lot of friends. The manipulator can come in and offer to be that friend and can work to build up the confidence of their target. As they are doing this, the target will feel indebted to the manipulator and will be more likely to do what the manipulator wants.

- **Those who respond to guilt**: Guilt can be a powerful motivator, and a good manipulator will be able to use this to their advantage. These targets want to be helpful and do not want to feel guilty for not doing something that they should. A manipulator can play the victim card a little bit with this one, and they are sure to get this target to act the way that they want.

- **Those who like flattery**: If you are someone who likes to listen to flattery and will chase it down, then you will be a very easy target for a manipulator. All the manipulator will need to do in this situation is start adding in some flattery. They could spend time with you, compliment you often, and just be overall nice to you. These actions will stroke your ego, and you will open yourself up to do what the manipulator wants.

- **Those who are empathetic to others**: This is a great option to go for as a manipulator. These people like to help others and are always falling for the next sob story they hear. They understand that people fall on hard times, and they want to be there to help. While their ideals may be altruistic, many people will take advantage of this. They simply need to make the target feel bad for them, such as telling them a sad story or letting them know that they, the manipulator, is used to this abuse. If they can do this properly, this kind of target will jump into helping them right away.

- **Those who become blinded by love**: Manipulators love this kind of target because they will be able to make them fall deeply in love. They will say and do all the right things to make the target believe that they are in love. The target believes that they are so much in love that the other person would never harm them.

While it is possible for anyone to be manipulated during their lives, there are some people who are easier targets than others. If you fall into one of the categories above, it may be time to make some changes before someone tries to manipulate you and take over your life. Remember that the manipulator is not willing to work harder than they need to manipulate the other person. If they feel that someone will be at least a little bit difficult to manipulate, they will pick someone else to target.

You Can't Change Your Manipulator

It is impossible to change your manipulator and to try to do this is just going to result in heartache and more issues in your life. However, you can make changes in yourself that will make things more difficult for the manipulator and perhaps make them go away.

The moment that you stop pleasing, complying, or cooperating with the manipulator is the moment that they will leave you alone. The manipulator does not want to work hard for the control, and if you start putting up a fight, then they will take off and look for someone else.

There are many targets who believe that they can change their manipulator. They want to stay around in the hopes that the manipulator will suddenly realize what is going on and will want to make a change. However, this is never going to happen. While there may be a few manipulators who are unaware of the tactics that they are using, most manipulators are skilled at what they are doing, and they have been working for a long time to perfect their techniques. These individuals will be impossible to change. Even when they are confronted and made aware of how they are hurting the target, they will not find the motivation to change.

Most manipulators can disguise their motives by hiding behind a lot of layers of lies. It is impossible to add on all these layers without knowing exactly what you are doing, and it is unlikely that they care that you think it is a bad thing. If they can maintain the control, they will be happy.

Since there are all these layers of lies that the manipulator must maintain, they will often use some tactics that are considered acceptable by society. This can just make it more confusing for the target. Some of the tactics that they may consider using include:

- The manipulator will resort to caring for and loving their target for a time. They will spend some time showing the target how much they care for them. They use this love as a bargaining tool to get the target to do what they want.

- The manipulator may try to overpower the target, sometimes making the target feel like the manipulator is the expert.

- The manipulator can try to show the target how generous they are. They will show the target that they care because they are helping them out in any way they can. They may say that they are doing something to help the target, or they are doing it for the target's own good.

One thing that you should consider is that it is not a good idea to ask a manipulator what their true intentions and motives are. You are not going to get an honest answer at all. The manipulator is a skilled liar, and they will be able to keep it all hidden. Often these questions will result in the manipulator getting defensive or angry towards you. Most manipulators have the idea that they deserve to do these things because they help them get to their goals, no matter what it takes.

Chapter 3. What Makes People Chat Without Thinking?

On the main one hand, information overload has made us overstimulated and we think it is a growing number of difficult to stop the inner chatter. On the other, prolonged silence quickly opens the hinged door to feelings we may be trying to keep buried, egg emptiness, harm, frustration, etc.

However, if at the various other ends of the scale you have an emotionally intelligent one who can manage their emotions and use words appropriately, it's no wonder they are frequently headhunted by the most reputable companies.

10 Main Great Things About Having High Psychological Intelligence

People Enjoy Working With/for You

Emotionally intelligent people don't harass their staff or bully their colleagues. They understand how to obtain others to accomplish what they need without resolving to arrogance or aggression. Being versatile and open to suggestion, they make great leaders or colleagues.

People Easily Open to You

Being empathic, emotionally smart people can listen in to others' emotions, so they easily understand others' point of view or the conditions which may have led them to do certain things.

You Certainly Are a Master of Your Feelings in Any Situation

The ability to identify, understand, and manage your emotions means you'll continually be a step forward over others with regards to responding to challenging situations. Besides, getting responsible for your emotions can help you manage stress better.

You Resolve Conflicts Easily

The secret to successfully resolving conflicts is to deal with them prior to the situation gets beyond control. Your ability to manage your emotions, and conveniently understand those of others, along with triggers that may possess led to them, makes it possible to respond to someone's behavior in a manner that will diffuse a potentially difficult situation.

Because your interpersonal skills are good, you feel relaxed around people and so are not quickly thrown off balance in unpredictable and difficult situations, or with unfriendly or hostile individuals openly.

You Easily Turn Into a Leader

Emotionally intelligent folks have most of the traits of highly effective leaders: they are empathic, confident, communicative, positive, and supportive.

You Can Work Anywhere, With Anyone

Great people skills, empathy, and social awareness imply that you will be able to work well and get most from every situation even under difficult circumstances or in a foreign culture.

You Get Yourself a High-Paid Job Easily

Being probably the most sought-after abilities at work, high emotional cleverness can help you get the job of your dreams.

You Don't Carry Out or Say Things You Later Regret

Knowing that you need to understand and process your feelings before releasing them, implies that you will only act once you've had an opportunity to consider the problem. Sometimes, all it takes is having a few minutes to believe things over and present yourself a chance to calm down and measure the circumstance, before making the final decision.

If there are occasions you are too embarrassed to take into account because of what you said, or did, it's probably because at the time you didn't have or didn't use your emotional cleverness, as a total consequence of which you made decisions you resided to regret.

You Are a Valued Friend and Confidant

Psychological intelligence skills are as useful outside work just, as some of your most significant emotions and decisions happen outside the workplace, egg with your family, in your passionate relationships, together with your friends, children, etc.

You Are Fulfilled

Having a successful career and being accomplished personally means you should have lived your life to the fullest.

So, through inside your feelings, behavior, and interpersonal relations, emotional intelligence includes a major effect on the standard of your life.

To continually cultivate and enhance these skills, you should never go wrong on your:

Self-Awareness

Be constantly in touch with your feelings and figure out how to listen in to them.

Social Skills

Cultivate your communication abilities rather than underestimate the charged power of words. Besides, to become highly empathic, you possess to try to develop humility. Although becoming humble isn't easy in a society which encourages individuality and competition, ability to admit your limitations and mistakes openly, are characteristics of a true leader.

Emotional Regulation

Figure out how to control your strong emotions, particularly negative ones, and never act on impulse. Practice this by thinking about something that will make you feel hurt, angry, or exploited. Sit down with the feeling, feel the humiliation, or anger, "digest" it, and only once you have calmed down "respond" to the individual or scenario that made you feel that way.

Chapter 4. Manipulation of the Mind Through NLP

Here, we will look at NLP techniques that can be used to influence others in social situations and in ordinary interpersonal dynamics. Here, we will discuss techniques that use those concepts to help you get what you want.

Embedding Commands in the Statements That You Make

When you want someone to comply with a request that you are making, you can make statements in such a way that they include specific commands.

For instance, if you want to ask your friend to schedule a lunch date with you, you can phrase your request as a command instead of a question. So, instead of saying, "can we have lunch sometime this week?" you say, "let's have lunch this week."

It may seem like the same request either way, but the reactions you'll get from those two statements are completely different. The first one is a question, so there is room for a yes or no answer. Here, your friend is highly likely to turn you down even if scheduling your lunch date is only slightly inconvenient.

When you say, "let's have lunch this week," it feels like a commanding statement. This kind of phrasing primes your friend to feel as though the question of whether or not you are going to have lunch is a foregone conclusion, and now the only thing that's left, is for the two of you to figure out the logistics. So, in his mind turning you down is going to feel like an insurmountable task, and he will be more inclined to adjust his schedule to accommodate your lunch date.

There is also a greater sense of urgency in the second request that there is in the first one. Even if your friend is generally inclined to have lunch with you at some point in the future, the first request increases the chances that your friend will try to bargain and schedule your date further away. The second request, on the other hand, creates the impression that the date needs to happen as soon as possible, so in your friend's mind, it will register as a major priority.

There are many other ways that you can conceal commands in the statements that you make. This is especially done in sales and marketing; salespeople are trained to use hidden commands to upsell you when you go to their stores. For example, when you've just bought a shiny new electronic gadget, if you are dealing with a well-trained salesperson she will ask you "what accessories do you want with that?" instead of "do you want any accessories with that?"

In the first statement, there is the implication that you must get at least one or more accessories, but in the second statement, there is the implication that accessories are generally optional. If you have a few bucks left, you are more likely to consider spending them on an accessory if you heard the first question than you are likely to do it if you heard the second question.

Creating the Illusion of Choice

The illusion of choice is also a common NLP technique, and it can be used to condition someone to select a specific option (or one option from a limited set of choices) while conditioning him to think that he has several choices at his disposal. The illusion of choice can be used in romantic relationships, in parenting, in the workplace, and in lots of other social dynamics.

For example, let's say you walk into a restaurant, and you get seated, then your waiter walks over and asks "which wine would you like, red or white?" you might go ahead, check the wine list, and order something that's within your price range. However, if the waiter comes over and asks, "What would you like to drink?" or "would you like some wine?" you would be more inclined to turn him down.

The difference here is that in the first instance, the waiter has limited your options, and he has primed you to think that you have a choice. You will be choosing whether you want a red or white wine, and you may even have to choose between different brands and different price points. Since you are presented with a fixed set of choices, your mind still thinks that you are acting on your own free will, so you don't feel as though you have been manipulated.

On the other hand, when the waiter asks what you would like to drink, or if you would like some wine, your options aren't restricted. So, mentally, you wouldn't feel at all uncomfortable if you just asked for some water, or if you ordered a cocktail instead.

Some savvy marketing experts can add a twist to the illusion of choice technique to make people more inclined to select one option over another. If for instance, there are two things to pick from, and a salesperson wants you to pick the one that profits him the most, he may introduce a third "decoy option" to steer you towards the choice he wants.

For example, restaurant menus often sell combined items at a lower price than they do individual items to make people think that they are getting a bargain when they order more items.

For example, a restaurant may list its menu items as follows: Burger—$2.30; Fries—$1.50; Burger & Fries—$3.30. Now supposing you walked into the restaurant planning only to have a burger. Once you look over the menu, you realize that you will "save" $0.50 if you selected the combo instead.

Strategic Use of the Words "but" & "and"

These two words may seem simple, but they have a lot of weight when they are strategically used in conversation.

You can use the word "and" at the beginning of all your sentences during the conversation to indicate agreeableness and to prime the other person to be more agreeable by extension. The "and game" is often used in improvisational theatre to help people generate free-flowing ideas, but in interpersonal conversations, you can use an iteration of that game to make the other person feel like they can open up to you.

It's very simple; when someone is done speaking, follow up their last sentence with the word "and," then add your own statement. For example, if your date says, "This steak is really delicious," you can follow that with "and it pairs well with this wine." This creates the impression that your minds are in sync, so the person will be more receptive to your ideas.

The word "but" on the other hand has the power to negate anything that comes before it in a sentence and to make the listener lend more weight on whatever comes after.

Let's take these two sentences as examples: If your friend told you "my brother is a very smart guy, but he can be difficult to deal with." you are more likely to think that her brother might not make great company because you will have a difficult time dealing with him.

However, if your friend says "My brother can be difficult to deal with, but he is a very smart guy" you are more likely to think that her brother might provide interesting company, and getting along with him might be slightly challenging at first.

The phrase that comes afterward seems to hold more significance than the one that comes before; so you can keep that in mind in cases where you have to deliver both positive and negative news, or in scenarios where you have to talk about something's negative and positive qualities.

For example, if you are selling a second-hand car, you are more likely to win over a customer by saying "the rear has a slight bump, but it gets good gas mileage" instead of saying "it gets good gas mileage, but the rear has a slight bump."

Reframing

Reframing is an NLP technique that is most used by salespeople to get their customers to change the way they perceive things. One of the most effective ways to change a person's mind is by altering their perception—reframing is the process that goes into altering people's perceptions.

Reframing involves taking a fact, a belief or conviction, and restating it so that your target sees the situation from an angle that he has never considered before. Reframing is a way of changing the meaning of something, so that it becomes more powerful or less powerful, depending on what it is you want to get out of the situation. Reframing often involves redefining something that your target things of as a problem, and making it seem like a challenge.

For example, when someone tells you, "Your idea is stupid." You can reframe that situation by saying, "Yeah, but it's also stupid not to consider all possibilities." In this case, you have taken the person's fear of seeming stupid, turned it around, and used it against him. So, in his mind, he feels like he will be betraying his own logic if he doesn't consider your idea.

NLP experts who work in sales often use the concept of "disruptive reframing" to make their products, services, and ideas seem more valuable to potential clients. Disruptive reframing refers to a persuasion technique where the audience's focus is shifted or disrupted in a way that makes certain things seem more manageable.

Disruptive reframing is often used in car adverts. For example, instead of saying that a car costs $15,000, the dealer may state that it costs "$3000 per year" or "$250 per month." A more creative dealer may break it down further by claiming that the same car costs $8 per day. He might even try to completely change the frame and take money out of the equation by claiming that you can get the car "for the price of two cups of coffee per day."

In this example, the salesperson isn't lying; he is just reframing the facts in a disruptive way. He knows that a $15,000 price tag may seem intimidating for a person with an average income and many expenses, so he takes away his customers' concerns by equating that amount of money to something small that people spend money on without thinking twice.

Having the Last Word in a Discussion

The last words are extremely powerful. There is a reason why people are obsessed with "famous last words" of historical figures. Just like those famous last words sum up the lives of great men and women in history, the last word in a conversation sums up the entire conversation. Even if you had differing opinions during a conversation, and even if you "agreed to disagree" with the other person, having the last word makes your point stronger in his or her mind.

Some people tend to let others have the last word in arguments because they just want the argument to end, but that is unwise. Manipulators who understand NLP can use last words to steer you in the direction in which they want you to go.

Even in casual talks, manipulative people will insist on saying the last thing because, from an anthropological and psychological standpoint, it somehow implies that they are higher than the other person in the dominance hierarchy, and therefore their word carries more weight. Think about formal settings (such as boardroom meetings, political rallies, etc.), the highest-ranking person is almost always the last one to speak, and he or she is the one who dismisses the meeting, by literary giving others permission to leave the room and go out and do something else.

You can use NLP to exert dominance over somebody in the long run by having the last word every time you talk to them. If you hold collegial meetings with your coworkers (those who are at your peer level), you can create the impression that you are the "alpha" of the group by always being the one that has the last word.

The Use of Questions

NLP experts love this technique because it enables them to hijack someone's thought patterns without them realizing it. Questions are so effective at steering people's thoughts; they are often used in mass media, in political rhetoric, and in many other areas. Questions have a way of forcing the target to look at things from the point of view of the manipulator.

Questions allow you to make a statement without making it. You may have encountered news headlines like "Are eggs bad for you?" or "Is fossil fuel the only viable energy source?" In such instances, the writers of these articles want to convey a controversial point of view that they have (e.g. "eggs are bad for you" or "the benefits of fossil fuels outweigh the environmental concerns") but because they know that these ideas may face pushback, they choose to present them as questions so that they seem ambiguous.

You can use this technique in interpersonal relationships. For example, if you are trying to talk someone out of a certain idea or point of view, you can do it by saying "You seem to raise some good points but ask yourself this question." When you drop in the question, your target will have no choice but to ponder on the idea that underlies that question. You have effectively taken control of his thought process, and you have pushed it in a direction that is favorable for you.

Using the Word "Don't"

NLP experts can use the word "don't" as a decoy to steer people's thoughts towards a certain direction in order to influence their emotions and actions.

The human mind has a difficult time comprehending negatives. In many cases, it processes negative statements the exact same way it processes positive statements.

If someone tells you "think about elephants," images of elephants are going to pop into your mind.

If someone else tells you "don't think about lions," images of lions are going to pop into your mind.

While your conscious mind can logically tell the difference between the positive and the negative statement, your subconscious mind cannot (remember that the subconscious uses a different linguistic system). So, if you tell someone not to focus on something, he will inevitably focus on it.

You can use the word "don't" as an NLP technique in almost all areas in life. If you want to nudge your spouse into thinking about your future subliminally, you can mention in passing how lucky you are that you don't have to think about those plans for a while.

For example, if you want your spouse to start thinking about buying a home, you can just pretend to be reading the business section of a newspaper and say something like "It looks like the housing market is still recovering. I'm glad we don't have to think about buying a home for now."

When you say that, your spouse won't be able to help it; he will start thinking about buying the house because that's what his subconscious mind will tell him to do.

Using the Word "Means"

Our brains are wired to find meaning in the information that we take in and find links and associations between different ideas and concepts. This is crucial for our survival; the brain creates "maps of meaning" for the sensory information that we gather so that when we encounter that information, later, we know exactly what we are dealing with. This explains why children as so inquisitive; for the brain to function properly, everything we encounter needs to hold some meaning, so children can help it but ask for an explanation for everything that they cannot understand.

If you want to persuade someone, you can be able to do it by providing meaning to the information that is available to them and by linking what they are thinking with what you want them to think. To do this, you must use the word "mean" as frequently as you need to during your conversation with the person whom you are trying to influence.

For example, when you are pitching an idea to a client, you can finish your presentation with lines such as "hiring me means you get the best services" or "using our services means fast results, which means more money for you."

However, even without using the word "means," you can condition a person to associate certain ideas with certain feelings. This technique is often used in advertising to link products with positive experiences. For example, all Coca-Cola adverts showcase happy people doing exciting things because their marketing experts want you to believe that "Coca-Cola means happiness."

Using the Word "Because"

When you use the word "because" in a sentence, it indicates to the person you are talking to that "all questions have been answered," and they are more likely to give you what you want without bombarding you with lots of follow-up questions.

The word "because" starts almost all sentences that are used to answer the question "why?" So, when you preemptively use the word "because" in your statement, the person you are talking to will subconsciously feel as though all of his "why" questions have been addressed.

For example, when you ask your friend, "I need to borrow your car to go to the mall." He is more likely to have a follow-up question than if you had told him, "I need to borrow your car because I have to go to the mall." When he hears the first sentence, he will feel as though you haven't addressed your reason for borrowing his car. When he hears the second sentence, he will as if the latter part of the sentence (going to the mall) explains the former part of the sentence (borrowing the car).

Chapter 5. Mental Control with NLP for Love and Relationships

In this chapter, we will discuss how NLP can be beneficial to healthy relationships. We will learn what truly good and fulfilling relationships are based on and built upon. We are going to explore techniques that can be used to strengthen relationships as well as those which can help us in establishing healthy relationships. There are many factors that play a role in good relationships. We are going to discuss the importance of our mental health and readiness prior to entering any partnership, or relationship, and possible outcomes associated with having and not having these factors.

We all want and need certain things. There are basic needs for all of us and one of the most crucial ways in which we can have our basic emotional needs met is with healthy relationships. We all want to be loved. We all want to be desired and needed. We all long for compassion and understanding. All of these can be acquired in good and healthy partnerships. Likewise, a bad relationship can be devastating. Most of us carry around baggage, such as negative emotions, fear, and anxiety from previous unhealthy relationships and this can place barriers between us and others when we find ourselves in new relationships. True fulfillment usually can only be found in the emotional qualities within our personal relationships.

Every good relationship begins with a clear and comfortable frame and state of mind. Maturity of both parties is a factor as well as timing. Your goals and wants to need to be compatible with the person which you want as a partner. Your values and beliefs need to match. These ideas and characteristics are tangible and very important in the overall health of any relationship. If you find yourself in a great relationship, the benefits are numerous. You will gain confidence and feeling of self-worth that can't be matched. Just as important, you must remember to also transmit this to your partner. You should always treat your partner in the exact ways in which you wish for them to treat you. In doing this, and having this knowledge, you can know what it is that your partner wants. You just need to see what it is that your partner is doing and take it from there.

Before we can be the kind of partner we should, we must first be good within ourselves. If you enter a relationship, while you have self-doubt or internal difficulties, you are entering a partnership that is doomed from the start. A perfect couple consists of two people who can function well as individuals but function as a partner just as well, if not better. This is the first step in entering any relationship. You must be good with yourself. This is a must and shouldn't ever be compromised. The second important point that needs to be addressed is you must establish what, or who, it is that you desire. This is your own personal decision based on your personality, desires, ideologies, and belief system. It does not matter what others believe you need or what you think you should have. At the end of the day, what matters is what you want.

The next part of entering a good relationship is timing. This isn't just important to you, but it's also important with your partner. Are you looking for "Mr. Right" or "Mr. Right Now?" Are there things going on currently in your life that may prohibit your success in the relationship? Are these things, not only able to hinder you, but are they able to hinder your partner as well? Timing is important and crucial to the longevity of the relationship. If you are a point in your life where there are other priorities that take precedence with you, you should wait until those priorities shift and you are able to become capable of making your partner the priority that he or she deserves.

Once you have decided what it is that you want, have concluded that now is the time for you to enter into a relationship, and have covered all of your predetermining factors, now you can begin to open up to the possibilities of finding the right person. Here is when rapport becomes important. What is rapport? It's basically your similarities and likeness with someone with whom you are interested in entering a relationship with. It's also the establishment of trust with that person. With rapport, there are many individual factors that can be used for determining compatibility. Some of these are personality types, values, beliefs, culture, political ideologies, interests, religious beliefs, and so on. Of course, there are also physical characteristics, such as gender and body types, that need to be considered. However, some characteristics can't be overaccentuated because it will lead to mimicking the other and can cause a loss of rapport.

It's crucial that the rapport which is established in the beginning, and the reasons for your attraction to your partner, and his or her attraction to you, be kept at the forefront of each partner's minds throughout the relationship. It all too common for people to enter relationships with guns blazing, meaning being the perfect partner, only to begin to relax and change once the relationship has been established. One partner, or both, will use all available techniques to get the other to enter into a relationship but, once they are in that relationship, the other partner believes he or she can tone down what it was they were doing in the beginning. This is one of the most common reasons for relationships ending. Keep in mind, the reasons for someone falling for you are the same reasons that will make them want to stay with you. If you remove the reasons for their attraction, they have no reasons to stay with you. Often, we see children born of relationships used as new reasons, but this does not work. This leads the partnership to morph into, what be, a business relationship. There will be no real emotional connection in the relationship and, even though that couple may remain together, they will lack the comforts and fulfillment of needs in which they desire.

Now you have identified what you want, making sure the timing is right, and have met that special someone. Now, what do you do? You need to make sure that your partner feels the same about you. There are several ways in which a person can see that he or she is loved by the other. These ways should be identified at the relationships beginning. A few methods are by what the other person buys and places he or she takes you. There are also things such as the way in which they touch you, the looks they give, or what they say. Identification of these is important as they can be used to gauge the continuance of love throughout the relationship.

The best way to determine how you can best assure your partner that you love him or her is by doing for them what they tend to do for you. For instance, most likely if your partner puts her arm around you at times to assure you of her love and affection, you can bet that if you do the same, she will believe that you do love and appreciate her. We don't tend to do things to or for others, especially those whom we care about the most, that we wouldn't want to be done to us. Although this is commons sense, it's also a great method to gauge or determine how your significant other is feeling about you. As the relationship progresses, this will come naturally and will take much less conscious effort. Just be sure to not allow these things to stop just because the relationship is no longer new.

NLP has devised a few strategies to determine areas in relationships. Areas such as attraction, love, and desire are all strategized with NLP techniques. First, you must know your partner. This means that you should know what those subtle gestures and tones of voice your partner will display depending on how he or she is feeling. Know what your partner fears and what he or she wants. You will pick up ideas as to how to carry these things out simply by learning your partner. Be sure to never use this knowledge for manipulation. There isn't a positive outcome in relationships where manipulation takes place.

One technique you can use to ensure that your partner is in love with you and wants you is to temporarily remove yourself from his or her presence. This does not mean that you can tell your wife that you are going to the store for a lottery ticket only to not return for a week. However, in short time frames, absence can signal want or lack thereof. Just like the cliché, absence makes the heart grow fonder; this is built on the same premise. When using these kinds of tactics, please never overuse them. Here is some advice. If you are an insecure person needing constant approval and reassurance that you are loved, you should take care of that issue prior to ever entering a serious relationship. If not, you are not going to be a good partner and, if your shortcoming does not end the relationship, it could lead it to become a codependent partnership or, at the very least, a very unhealthy relationship. Again, you must first make sure that you are a good candidate for entering into a relationship prior to taking that next step.

Previously, we discussed those who are in sales and tactics which they can use in order to lead someone into a purchase. With relationships, you are not simply selling yourself to another and then the job is over. It's a continuing process forever. Never relax and believe that you have your partner and he or she isn't going anywhere no matter what you may or may not do. This mistake has been made countless times by many divorcees. You should always be selling yourself, your worth, your compassion, and your desire for your partner.

Now, we are going to look at the real world and all it gives us. As much as most of us wish it were, life isn't perfect. Regardless of what good we may do or how good of a person we may be, life will often provide us with the short end of the stick. When we would like milk and honey, sometimes we get vinegar and stale bread. That's just the way it is. It isn't going to change. So, the best that we can do is better prepare ourselves so that we can handle the difficult situations as they come. With relationships, there is no difference. We may be a great person, but things happen. We can know our partner perfectly, be the most affectionate and caring person, and have the utmost consideration for our significant other but that may fall short if given the right elements.

The most common reason given for divorce is what is known as "irreconcilable differences." What is this exactly? Webster defines it as "inability to agree on most things or on important things." It isn't suggesting that one or the other partners are inadequate or bad. It's simply that, for whatever reason, they find themselves disagreeing. First, did they have these disagreements when they first entered the relationship? Hopefully, they didn't. If the relationship was established properly, there must be another reason for these differences.

Both partners were independently ready for a relationship. They each chose their partner carefully and paid attention to every detail, no matter how benign. Both did their very best at pleasing the other and showed a great deal of compassion and love. So, what's the issue here? Many of us have witnessed relationships just like this. Both people are independently great as individuals. Both are loving and compassionate. Both appeared to be perfect fits for the other and they seemed to get along great and really loved one another. So, what happened to them and their relationship? I've seen couples divorce and it made me think that, if they didn't make it, the rest of society is doomed.

Think of this; You meet someone at the beach or any spot you can imagine. You are both at that exact place at that exact time. You may both have everything in common too. However, both you and the other person took different routes to that spot and lived through different circumstances while on the way. Even though you both find yourselves to be at the same point, and with the same characteristics, you took different paths there. This means that it's likely that you are not both going to react or respond to every event the same and those events may lead you to go in different directions. Another way to look at this; You may both like the same sports team. The difference is why each of you has this opinion of that team. One of you may be a graduate from that university, while the other just picked last season's champions. This probably means that the alumnus of the school is less likely to decide that he or she no longer favors that team. There are infinite ways to look at this. Regardless of the possible ways, the ending remains the same. What does this mean? Are we all just simply at life's mercy and subject to emotional trauma at the drop of a hat? Not exactly. Although we may not be able to change the situation when finding ourselves here, but we can at least know why. First, don't give up. Do whatever you can in order to carry both you and your partner through the tough spot in your relationship and you may find that you both were able to beat the odds and remain together.

Let's look at what it means to have taken different routes. Obviously, the previously mentioned scenarios were only metaphors. The location isn't an actual place but a specific state of mind and life situation. Regardless of the spectrum of commonalities you and your partner may or may not have, you both will respond, and react, to things differently. One of you may be able to brush something off, such as a traumatic event, but the other isn't able to do that. Let's look at this. Both you and your wife have a religious faith. This is one of the main commonalities you found of yourselves that led to your relationship. Later down the road, your wife either endures a traumatic event, or meets an influential person, either causing a dramatic shift in her religious ideologies. Now, what was once the main glue that kept you together, has deteriorated to where there is no more left. Not only does she no longer agree with your religious faith, her newfound beliefs totally contradict what you believe. What do you do when faced with this situation? Both of you are strongly holding to your individual beliefs and not willing to waiver. Both accuse the other of being naïve. Neither of you are bad people, but you are no longer finding the same rapport you once had.

You both joined into the relationship only after taking the proper steps and exercised due caution in choosing the other as a mate. Even though this was done, life didn't care about that. Circumstances led to the separation of you and your partners beliefs and both of you are much too committed to your independent ideas to compromise them. Therefore, you now are at constant odds and the negativity within the relationship grows stronger each day. One day, it will lead to resentment and even hate. You have taken the necessary steps in attempting to salvage the relationship to no avail. So, as the very last resort, you decide to part ways. This happens every day.

Just like the baggage we carry due to prior bad relationships; we carry lessons learned and individual ways of dealing with certain issues which are based on these lessons. It's one of the ways in which we are individual but is also a way in which we can find ourselves at odds with another. The best thing to do is know what and how things are going, and this can give you a good idea as to what is about to come.

To conclude this chapter, NLP is extremely important and beneficial in the relationship. This isn't just with the beginning of the union but throughout its entirety. You must first know yourself and then using NLP you can learn your partner. Knowing your partner can prove invaluable in maintaining a healthy and long relationship. Also, the relationship will be much more fulfilling to both parties. Remember that serious and personal relationships prove beneficial in many areas in life and isn't limited to just the partnership. It's beneficial for both of you as a couple, as individuals, and as part of society.

Chapter 6. Advanced Manipulation Methods: Love Bombing, Foot-In-The-Door, NLP Mirroring

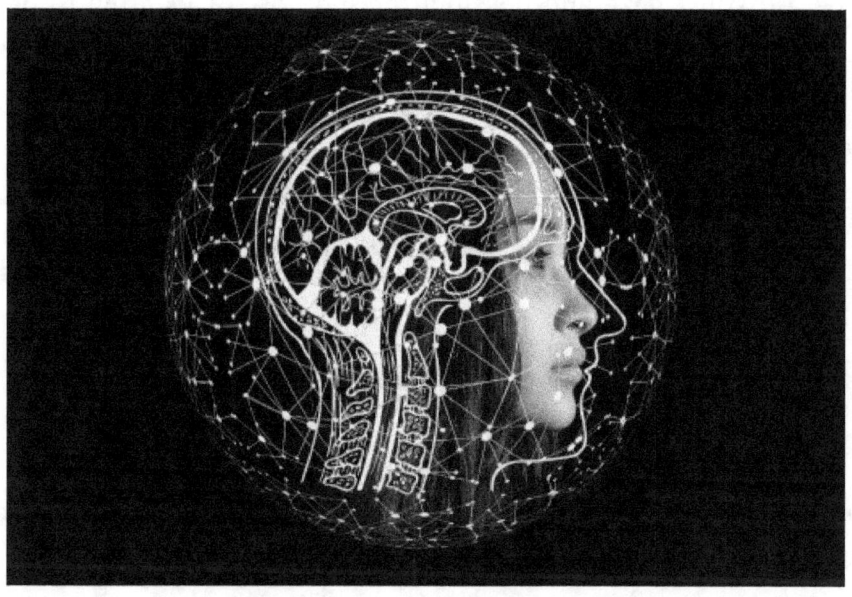

One of the downfalls of technology is the loss of true communication. We no longer have in-person communication as was done years ago. We can simply send a text or email in mere seconds and get the message to whomever we are communicating with. Even with the telephone, there was the ability to have some communication beyond simple words, but we don't use this often anymore. Most of our communicating now is done with text and must be read. Have you ever wondered what is lost with this? Communication, real communication that is, is only partially words. Most communicating is done by methods we commonly don't even think about.

Most of what we communicate to another person is done through tone and body language. Most of us have heard of this before. However, with just a little common sense, one can see how this works. Take for instance someone who is being standoffish to you during a conversation. What would that person's posture be? More than likely, he or she will be standing a bit taller and will have his or her arms crossed. There will also be a distinct gaze and possibly the look of not wanting to be there talking with you. Parents, if you have teenagers you know exactly what this looks like. You will see the rolling of the eyes, tapping of the toes, and the sporadic checking of the time on a watch or phone. Even though your teenager hasn't said "okay dad but I'm tired of listening to you and I've got to go," you knew that was the case. Why is this? It's because getting that point across didn't require a single word. It simply took a posture and a slight attitude.

This is one technique of finding out if the person you are talking to is sincere or interested in what you have to say. There is a warmth associated with communicating with someone who possesses a pleasant demeanor. It's much easier to find that someone is being dishonest with you if you can see them during your conversation. This isn't possible when the only way that you are communicating is by using written words. What I've just described deals with the topic of this chapter. That is neuro-linguistic programming. Neuro refers to the mind. Linguistic refers to language. Programming refers to how the mind and body function together in communication. You can think of NLP as a language of the mind and body. NLP does have a reputation of being associated with those who manipulate. This is in a negative sense. So, as you continue your journey in learning the art of persuasion and mind control, be cautious about what you share with others. You don't want to establish a bad reputation as being a trifling person.

NLP shouldn't be seen in a negative fashion. Think of it as a game of Chess. However, rather than there being a winner and loser, there are two winners. Think of what happens when a salesperson makes that sale. Hopefully, there are two winners. The salesperson has made the sale and gained a profit. The customer made a purchase and gained something that he or she desired. Even though the salesperson used persuasion in making the sale, it led to both parties winning. One way to see this is by looking at ecology. The ecosystem is balanced and allows for all parts to come out on top. When there is an introduction of someone new into the system, will it benefit the system, is a way in which this can be viewed. So, it will be best if you view NLP and the persuasion of someone else in this light.

We have discussed how those who manipulate or persuade need to be good at mindfulness and be able to easily connect with others. Here is another trait one need possess in order to successfully persuade others. This works with the other characteristics in unison. You need to know people and their desires and fears. You also need to know what they are truly saying when you are talking to them. People are always saying one thing while meaning another, also known as lying, and this is how you can minimize their ability to use this to pull a fast one on you. Studies have shown that, when communicating, 7% of this is done with words. The other 93% is done using NLP. Most will agree that the most important aspects of a conversation are with the 93% that are not words. A good communicator will have mastered non-verbal communication techniques.

Surprisingly, NLP isn't just when you are talking with someone else. It's also important for your self-communicating. This is inner communication. That's right; We don't just think about, or ponder on, different things. Our inner communication is constructed of different images, sounds, and feelings. If you are feeling tense, you may be able to figure out why by using this technique. You only need to begin to turn your attention inward and begin to look around within. We are not going to discuss how you can pick up on different things within yourself with NLP in this book. The importance of knowing this lies with one rule that remains steadfastly true. If you can do something to yourself, or recognize something within yourself, you will be able to do that with others. This is where we are going here.

NLP is a new concept, technique, and topic of study. Although relatively new to humans, its practice has been around for a long time. Have you ever heard to never look some animals in the eye? Have you been told not to smile at some primates because they see that as a form of aggression or threat? Their communication is done without spoken words and is part of NLP. With us, the study of NLP began during the early 1970s. At the University of California, Santa Cruz, a group of scientists, doctors, and therapists began to study how body language and things such as tone factored in with communication. They developed a practice called modeling which is the process of discovery in transformative communication. Basically, modeling is looking at the successes of others and creating your process based on their strategies and techniques. This is the method of teaching others about NLP.

There are a few principles with NLP. The first principle is the saying "the map is not reality." What this means is personal perception being your truth. To further explain, our perceptions are our own realities, but these are individual and differ from person to person. What someone else may see as reality may not be the same in your opinion. What we see, or perceive, is our reality regardless of what others think. This is because we all perceive and process things differently. The most important thing here is that we represent what we perceive well within ourselves and our realities are useful for us. Or as the saying goes, "be true to thine self."

Another principle is that you must know your outcome. This is extremely important. It needs to be well thought out, useful and must comply with the following criteria. It must be stated positively in that you need to focus on what you want, not what you don't want. Know which senses will cue to you know when you have been successful. These senses are sight, hearing, smell, touch, and taste. They must be acquired under appropriate conditions. They must be achievable, so you need to make sure that you will have access to the appropriate resources when needed. They must be ecological as previously mentioned in this chapter. This means the outcome needs to be, or should be, balanced. The outcome needs to be worthwhile. Lastly, you need to be ready to take the needed action and not procrastinate.

The next principles are sensory acuity and behavioral flexibility. We have looked at these also, but they need to be mentioned here. This is our ability to read the cues sent by others in their body language and other non-verbal cues. We then need to be ready to change our tactics accordingly. If what we are doing isn't working, try some other tactic. This requires more than knowledge of the process. It requires absolute attention to the other person and the ability to immediately change direction while doing it all correctly.

The last one is the physiology of excellence. This is your current state at that given time. You need to be relaxed and comfortable. If, for some reason, you are not in this state, its best to wait until you are. For instance, if you are too cold, you can use anchors to change this in order to make yourself feel relaxed. A way to do this is through mapping, which we will discuss further in this chapter.

There are some techniques with NLP that we will now discuss. The first is the calibration. This is both internal and external but, for our purposes, we are going to look at external. This is relating to, what is known as, sensory acuity. What this means is the ability of perception with others. Through their appearance, we can understand what they are most likely thinking or feeling at that point. First, we recognize the sensory activities of someone else as it relates to their feelings. A few ways which this can happen are in being aware of their tone of voice, skin tone, and breathing patterns. As you notice the changes in their state, you can tailor your responses accordingly. This is a good skill for salespeople. It's a good ability for influencing others and for persuasion. This is also good for spotting deception.

The second technique is anchoring. This be synonymous with the association. Anchoring is matching a sound or touch with some state. The ability to anchor another person can be done openly or covertly. There are some negative effects of anchoring.

An example of this can be seen with those suffering from post-traumatic stress disorder. Those individuals may have formed unhealthy associations, or anchors, that lead to flashbacks. For example, a war veteran hears a firecracker and associates that with gunfire. This is an auditory anchor. Other anchors include visual anchors. This can be something like seeing a certain symbol leading you to remember an event. For instance, seeing a shirt with your former school's logo printed on it. This may lead you to start thinking about your time in school. There is the olfactory anchor which is associated with certain smells. You may smell something sweet and that leads you to want to go to the candy store. Or you smell a perfume and it makes you think of a former girlfriend. Being well versed in anchoring gives you the advantage of being able to use these anchors in leading someone to think in a certain way or to remember an event.

Lastly, there is mapping across. Usually, this is done with the use of sub modalities. What are these? These are the finer details of our internal experiences. Here is an example. You think of someone that you are particularly fond of and, after thinking about them, you picture them in a pleasant fashion. The overall picture of that person is modality. The way in which you are picturing that person in your mind is the sub modality. Obviously, this isn't limited to people or things. The possibilities are endless. Again, mastery of this can prove to be extremely beneficial. Sub modalities can be kinesthetic, auditory, visual, and so on. In mapping across, we can use this to identify an experience where there isn't another resource available. You can link two experiences together. You have one experience where there isn't a resource and another where there is, and you link the two together. This is by identifying the similarities of modalities of each experience. This technique is a bit more difficult and will take some practice. Just as with anchors, we can use our knowledge and understanding of mapping across to our benefit when trying to persuade someone.

If you want to become successful using NLP, you will need to practice. This is a never-ending process of constant learning and skill acquerment. Remember, this isn't only to persuade others but can also be very beneficial for our own mental health. Having suggested this, let's look at some techniques which have been proven to work well with NLP and persuasion.

First, we need to understand the differences between commands and questions. This is important when dealing with others because, not only can we use this for persuasion, we can also use it in order to change direction depending on how those we are dealing with is responding. Let's look at open-ended questions versus closed. If I were to ask you a question like this, "what is your favorite color?" You could answer with any color imaginable. If I were to ask "what is your favorite color, red or blue" this will lead the answer to be one of the two. I may be trying to get you to say red and you may say blue, but I've limited the possibilities to only 2. There is also tonality. You need to be aware of the differences in voice tones and the meaning of each. Usually, demands are made with high tones and questions with low tones. Knowledge of this can help when dealing with someone who will become standoffish if they believe you are attempting to lead or control their thoughts.

There is also a technique of utilizing negative commands. This is much like "reverse psychology." We tend to do things which we are told not to do, and you can use this knowledge to your advantage. For instance, if I were to tell you to not think about pigs. What are you most likely going to think about at that exact moment? That's right; You are going to think about a pig. Here is an example of how to use a negative command rather than just a command. If I were to tell you to take your time, that's a command. However, if I were to suggest to you that you don't need to hurry, that's a negative command. Both suggest the same thing, but one may work over the other. This is, of course, totally dependent on your audience and thus you need to be knowledgeable of what you are attempting to do.

Another technique to use leads to creditability. What is meant here is you need to use things that will generate interest in others at the start. Also tailored to everyone, this can lead to successful persuasion. Here is an example, if I were to make up some fact that I was sure would generate great interest of the reader, and were to lead the book off with this fact, that person is more likely to continue reading what is written. Whether the fact, or statement, is true or not isn't important. It's best to always be honest. Including background information of whatever topic, you are discussing will usually generate greater interest by your target in the topic.

There is also, what is known as, the "swish" technique. This is primarily auditory and visual. This is the ability to change, reduce, or remove the trajectory of negative thoughts which may get in the way of your goals in persuasion. There is also, what is known as, the swish pattern. This is interchangeable with the swish technique. An example of this is the ability to recognize something that happened in the past and how the remembrance of this may cause someone to not do something in the future and the ability to change it. Using this technique allows you to not have to struggle with negative thought. This is because you can change thinking to lead to a more positive note.

In order to be successful in the swish technique, the following steps must take place. First, you need to identify the unwanted trigger and what thought it would lead to. Then, you need to have a replacement thought if it is required in that scenario. After identifying these, you need to know the best point in which to make the switch. This will differ depending on the person, the situation, and the outcome sought. Practice this technique until it becomes second nature to you. Don't attempt these techniques until you are sure that you are going to be successful. You can't half-way do any of these techniques. You will almost certainly be called out by the very person you are attempting to lead. Then your creditability will be destroyed, and you may just write off whatever you were attempting to be a lost cause and move on. There probably won't be any going back.

A traditional NLP process, known to improve some unwanted behaviors, is known as the six-step reframe. This can be used to change habits, behaviors, and even beliefs. Through the 6 steps, we can achieve success with NLP. Here are those steps. The first is identifying something that you don't want to feel or do. This is self-explanatory. The second is to find a way to establish communication with the part that is causing this unpleasant feeling. This can be carried out in various ways and each will be depending on the situation and its factors. After that, we need to find and visualize the positive intention or idea. Know the difference between the intention and the way in which you are going about getting it. You then need to find alternative ways in which you can get the outcome in which you intend. After that, you need to evaluate your new choices. Ask are they acceptable and better than what there were previously. There may need to be a little negotiation here because there may not be one single perfect solution. If you are unable to do this, return to finding alternative choices and rethink them. After all of this is complete, you need to judge the ecology of your choices and you should make sure that you deem them acceptable to the entire picture.

Let's look at a technique called "conflict integration." This is for conflict resolution. This is a good technique to do away with things such as bad habits, procrastination, and indecisiveness along with other conflicts. It also can create harmony within your mind. This technique is also intended for use with yourself and not others. Here is how to carry out NLP conflict integration. As with the others, first we need to identify the part creating unwanted behaviors. Then identify a part which is working in opposition. Bluntly speaking, identify the good and the bad parts. Then you need to create mental images of both. You can use anything which can metaphorically represent a part. Place your attention on one of the parts then move to the other. Ask each about their intentions. Remember this is metaphorically speaking. After this, identify the resources that each part has at its disposal. Here, you must merge both parts, the good and the bad, together as one. Then you create a third part, and this is both other parts combined. You must absorb the third part in deeply then follow this by a few moments of relaxing and taking everything in. The last thing to do is look at your future decisions and consider how you are going to approach them differently now that you have created the third part which should allow you to approach it in a better fashion.

The final technique is called the "belief change process." Here, you are working with sub modalities. This is a straightforward and simple process. Here, we begin by thinking about a belief within ourselves which we would like to not have. This belief should be limiting or prohibiting in nature. Then, we need to think of some belief that we previously had of yourself that is no longer true. For instance, you used to think of yourself as overweight and out of shape. Now you don't because you take care of your physical body. Now, change the sub modalities. Replace the old belief with the new one. The last part is to change a belief in something that you know to be the absolute truth with one that you want to be true. You know that an apple is either red or green. You know this to be an absolute fact. This is a true belief. Replace something like this with what you want to be true. Picture this in your mind. It may take a few tries but will work in the end.

To summarize NLP, along with what has been previously discussed in this chapter, it's also important to know that one core belief, or assumption, with NLP is that behind every behavior there is a positive intention. There are many benefits, beyond the ability to lead others, from practicing NLP. One of the best reasons for NLP is the changes it can lead us to make within ourselves. It can increase the speed in which we learn, make us great team leaders, provides us with behavioral flexibility, as well as many other beneficial outcomes.

Chapter 7. List of Errors That Can Make You Vulnerable to Manipulation

A manipulator manages to reach his goal by playing on the weak points of his victims. His flair and experience make him choose those who seem to be the least assertive in life or who are least able to defend themselves. If necessary, he can weaken the resistance of his victims by playing on their fears or their preconceptions.

The Manipulator First Attacks the Weak

The Observation

The weakness is a momentary situation that often comes from an unfavorable balance of power. This is the case, for example, when one is confronted by a disdainful superior, a representative of the order who notices an offense, or a big, threatening man covered with tattoos.

The weakness can also come from a deficient physical state related to illness, fatigue, or overwork. Even if it is momentary, this weakness is none the less real and perceptible by the manipulator.

The weakness can be of psychological origin. Thus, the one who feels inferior, less rich, less intelligent, less beautiful, or less capable than his interlocutor automatically places himself in a position of inferiority and weakness. A decrease in morale or a depressive state weakens the defenses and exposes him more fully to the attacks of the manipulators.

In any case, a state of weakness hinders self-assertion and the ability to defend oneself. Therefore, we must not let the manipulator take advantage of his superiority, giving him too hastily what he expects.

To Resist

When one feels weak, the solution is simple: you must not be reactive. It is urgent not to rush or make decisions that you will inevitably regret one day or another. As little as possible must be said or done and you must avoid making hasty decisions by postponing what the manipulator asks until later.

When one feels both manipulated and in a position of weakness, the way to do this is as follows:

- Begin by making the manipulator understand that his claim has been well understood.

- Then insist that one is not able to answer, for the moment, its requirements.

- Finally, finish the conversation as quickly as possible, while remaining polite.

"I understand that what you're asking me is important to you, but for the moment, I cannot answer it. Thank you."

"Thank you for thinking of me by making me the offer, but you see I am not able to make a decision. Goodbye."

"I understand that (reformulate their request), but I cannot. Excuse me." Then, leave as soon as possible!

When one feels weak or inferior, one must not flee shamefully. To do so would be an indicator of weakness that shows the manipulator that he can continue to harass us in peace. What is needed is to leave the interaction by operating a strategic retreat based on the following three actions: acknowledge receipt, defuse, and stop.

Acknowledgment means that we have understood their request. It's a question of being able to formulate it, with our words. This reformulation shows without question that we have fully understood what the manipulator has just told us. It does not allow the manipulator to take advantage of our misunderstanding or to insist heavily. The acknowledgment of receipt must be clear enough to indicate to the manipulator that we have understood what he wanted.

Defusing is simply saying (without getting lost in the details) that we are not in a condition or not able to respond to his request.

To stop is to quickly and politely interrupt conservation, without waiting for other answers. You must intend to stop the conversation without regret or remorse.

In a bar, a client tries to seduce the waitress who brings her order. After a few exchanges, he asks her "What time do you finish tonight?"

- Thank you for looking at my schedules (Acknowledge), but answering you is not part of my job. (Defuse)

- What a pity!

- Thank you, sir, and goodbye. (Stop)

A friend (who is a notoriously bad payer) asks you: "I do not know who to ask for money to pay for the repair of my car."

- Yes, I understand, this is not a pleasant situation. (Acknowledge)

- I will pay you back as soon as I have received the money I owe.

- Well, in these conditions, I think you'll get out of it. (Defuse)

- I hope.

- Bye! (Stop)

In operating a strategic retreat, sometimes we just put the problem back so that we don't need to deal with it while we may make a poor decision.

Remember

We cannot win every time! The strategic retreat at least avoids being manipulated once again. Think of a Type II manipulation in which you were in a weak position. Then, just imagine how you could have responded by using the three stages of strategic retreat.

The Manipulator Prefers Liabilities

The Observation

Passive people represent about a third of the people we meet in life. The manipulator appreciates them enormously because they do not allow themselves to react and do not know how to defend themselves; they are victims of choice for him. He finds them very easily and attacks them directly.

Generally, the passive person does not require anything because he is afraid of imposing himself. He prefers to be crushed underfoot rather than to say he is walking on his feet. He may be generous enough not to appear selfish or make disproportionate gifts to redeem imaginary or benign faults.

Passives are very discreet people who do not want to disturb. They are shy people who do not speak much or who spend their time apologizing. They are almost unable to refuse what they are asked for fear of appearing insensitive, antisocial, or unsympathetic. It is very difficult for them to talk about themselves and almost impossible to put themselves first.

They are often excessively helpful because they are more concerned with the interests of others than with their own needs. The problem with liabilities is that they forget their own existence and prefer to submit (forgetting themselves) rather than face conflict, disagreement, or judgment.

Passivity has deep roots that often go back to childhood. This won't be easily changed by reading a few lines. However, it is possible to explore a few tracks to help those who tend to behave in this way.

To Resist

To get out of the state of inferiority and loneliness in which he finds himself, the passive must be able to imagine that he is a human being just like others and that his opinion and desires are at least as valid as those men and women around him.

"Basically, all the other people I meet are like me. I am not the only one to suffer. Every man or woman I meet in life has experienced suffering. Everyone runs after happiness and seeks to satisfy his needs. But, at the same time, nobody has lived through the same things as me. No one knows what I live deeply, and no one knows exactly how much I suffer. All these people are different from me just as I am different from others. My opinions and desires are just as respectable as theirs. There are no superior or inferior people; there are only different people who are all equally respectable."

It is common to compare one aspect or detail of one's life with the same detail or the same aspect of another's life. One does not hesitate to say that one person is richer, more competent, more muscular, or more famous than another. We can compare cars or bank accounts, but we cannot compare globally between them.

If one evaluates someone in the entirety of their existence, nobody resembles anyone because each experience is different. We all move forward in life with a unique story that determines, to a large extent, the decisions we make at every moment. In these conditions, no one is like anyone and nobody can compare to anyone. We are as we are and there is neither shame nor pride in feeling different. We can (and must always) seek to improve, but in the end, we will never be anything but ourselves.

To accept others as they are is still the best way to accept oneself. To better understand all that this covers, here is a little exercise that we can do and redo for as long as we are surrounded.

Observe a person discreetly while repeating to you this series of sentences: "This person is like me, she also knew sorrow, sadness, despair... This person is like me and tries to avoid suffering... This person is like me, she needs to love and be loved... This person is like me and is looking for happiness... This person is like me, there are no two identical people... This person is like me, she is the only one to be who she is."

Repeat with different people until you feel a shift in your perception of others or yourself.

The Manipulator Wakes up Our Fears

The Observation

When a manipulator attacks someone who is neither weak nor passive, he still can achieve his goals by playing on the fear experienced by his victim. By playing this type of chord, the manipulator prevents the person from asserting himself and undermines his defenses as well as his ability to resist.

One of the uncontrollable fears that make us a designated victim is the fear of being hurt or hurting someone by denying them what they ask for. The manipulator spots wake up and use these kinds of fears to get us to do what he wants without us being able to defend ourselves.

The fear of giving oneself a bad image is blackmail that the manipulator also knows how to use, "Have you thought of what people will say if you ever do that?"

The fear of being judged often forces one to act against one's own desire.

One is also a victim of manipulation when one is afraid of offending the other: "You will not do that to me... You cannot refuse me this service... Listen, do it for me... I understand that you can refuse anyone, but not me... You cannot refuse to do that for your mother... Listen, I'm your friend all the same!"

Some manipulations are based on the fear of disappointing the other: "You know, I really need this money and I can't count on anyone but you... You can not disappoint me it's too serious for me."

Blackmail plays on the fear of losing someone, "If you do not do this for me, you do not love me."

But sometimes it is pride that makes us fall into the trap of manipulation, "You know, I could not ask this of just anyone, and I can only really count on you. I know you'll be discreet, won't you?"

It is very difficult to resist manipulations that play on the heartstrings of esteem, friendship, or love. The feelings we have for the manipulator should not play the role of the tree that hides the forest. It is not what binds us to the manipulator that is important; it is what he asks us or what he forces us to do.

To Resist

To oppose these different types of egocentric manipulations, here is the question that must immediately be asked:

"If someone broke away from me because I did not give in to the blackmail, he subjected me to, is that really someone who deserves my affection? On the contrary, is it not (at least for now) a vulgar type II manipulator who thinks only of his interest without worrying about mine?"

The answer is sometimes cruel, and it often takes courage to accept the evidence.

Ask yourself the following question: "The last time I gave in to this kind of manipulation, was the manipulator worth the price of my sacrifice?"

The Manipulator Uses Preconceptions

The Situation

Preconceived ideas are what everyone thinks about a situation. They are what is accepted by society and that no one would think to question (one must be honest, one should not lie, one must be generous). All these convictions represent an essential pillar of our education without which life in society would not be possible.

The manipulator plays on these beliefs (which always contain some truth) and diverts them to his advantage if we deny him what he asks, he will try to make us feel guilty by saying, "Those who do not know how to share are selfish!"

A kind grandmother created serious conflicts by saying with great conviction: "In the family, we can say everything." The one who was opposed to her was interrupted by this other idea: "You must respect my white hair."

According to their needs and circumstances, the manipulator will use one or another of these ready-made ideas to better enslave us. He can state a certain number of ready-made sentences: "It is not easy to refuse when you ask politely... We must always help others... We must trust... We must know how to be helpful... We must not leave people in need..."

He may also attempt to impose his will in holding forth: "You can never go wrong if... Always keep your word... It is easier to escape problems than to solve them..."

For the manipulator, ready-made ideas are an extraordinary means of pressure because they impose on us as universal truths that it would be out of place to question. These are truly conditioned reflexes that nobody doubts. And yet, this is what should be done because no ready-made idea can always prove to be accurate and under all circumstances.

Remember

Thus, the expression "he who does not attempt anything has nothing" can encourage someone who is hesitant to become self-employed or can manipulate someone who is hesitant to take drugs or to do any other stupid activity.

To Resist

When a manipulator uses a ready-made idea, one must not remain a prisoner of what he assures us with confidence. You must use common sense and question him (or ask yourself) by asking, "So what?" Then, depending on the answer obtained, the question must be repeated: "So what?" We continue like this until we escape manipulation.

"You should help me; I am your friend. (First idea ready.) And then?"

"With friends, it is normal to help each other. (The Second idea ready)"

"So what?"

"I need 1,000 €."

"I'm sorry, but I do not have that much money to lend."

"What about 500 €, could you?"

"Look, right now I cannot lend money to anyone and it has nothing to do with friendship. Okay?"

"Okay."

To overcome personal blockages that temporarily prevent us from resisting or opposing the manipulator, we can use the exercise by questioning ourselves.

Someone previously convinced you to help them and now you cannot do it anymore.

"I promised to help him."

"So what?"

"When one commits oneself, one must always keep one's word"

"And then?"

"Now I can't really help them anymore."

"So what?"

"He will not be happy."

"So what?"

"After all it's his problem and he did not give me the choice."

"So what?"

"I'll call him to explain the situation."

It is not the manipulator who makes us dependent, it is the ready-made ideas that we accept without questioning them. By questioning these ready-made ideas, the technique of "So what?!" can resist or defuse many types II manipulations.

Chapter 8. Skills to Be Developed to Become a Manipulator

It's easy to demonize manipulation when we're talking about someone else, like a cartoon villain, communist dictator, or the mean secretary from work. And the truth is, yes, manipulation can absolutely be used for evil, and it can do real damage.

It's not something to take lightly or play with if you don't know what you're doing. You wouldn't want to inflict damage. However, manipulation can be employed without destroying lives. Think of it like this: "bad" manipulation has the purpose to hurt other people, while "good" manipulation brings you advantages.

We're not here to debate the morality of manipulation, and I would even venture to say that if you're uncertain about whether you can, in good faith, engage in manipulation, then don't do it. At least, not until it's become clear where you stand. I would like to make it clear that it is not my aim to push anyone to do anything that contradicts their personal moral code. If you're cool with it, let us move forward and see what you can get out of this.

a) What You Can Achieve Through Manipulation

The first thing everyone wants to know, when it comes to manipulation, is what they can do with it. What can they achieve? What can they obtain from people that they couldn't before? Are there major advantages you can score, or are you just messing with people's minds for no reason other than your own sick sense of enjoyment?

The short answer is that yes, there are valuable things you can obtain from having the skills to manipulate those around you. These advantages can be in your personal life, in your professional life, or in any social setting, really. Whether you're trying to influence your friends or your boss, manipulation techniques will prove to be of tremendous help when you're trying to get what you want.

Establish Authority in Various Social Circles

When you know how to sweet talk people and make them do things for you, you become top dog. This goes for every social situation, whether you're in the workplace or within family dynamics. With the help of manipulation, you can make yourself look like the most authoritative person in that situation and the person everyone goes to for advice, instructions, etc.

Think about what it would be like to be the voice of reason in your family, instead of yielding to the reigning matriarch or patriarch? Grandpa's old fashioned and grandma's off her rocker and you shouldn't be forced to listen to them! Establish dominance and you will be the new leader of the clan.

Similarly, you can become the go-to guy at work. Ignore Dave, who is always getting in the way and undermining you. Butter up everyone else in the office—and if you happen to share something less than flattering about Dave, c'est la vie! You're better than him anyway, and so what if you had to pretend to like Meg from Accounting? Everyone likes you now and the whole office knows about that unfortunate, mysterious, and highly contagious rash Dave caught, so they avoid him, now. You can practice your evil cackle later.

Gain Social and Material Advantages

I know all major religions and general moral compasses say that lying is a bad thing to do but think of all the things it can get you! If you spin the tale in just the right way and play with someone's head just a little bit to make them feel guilty or pity you, you can gain social points, and even material advantages, if you play your cards right.

Now, I'm not talking about going to the food bank and pretending to be homeless to "score" a free meal, because that does not help anyone, and you're not exactly "gaining" anything, other than being a horrible person for no reason.

But if you've been gunning for that promotion at work, it can't hurt to butter up the boss a bit in order to get them to look upon you more favorably, does it? What if you started planting the idea in their head that you would be the perfect person for the job? Wouldn't that be a tremendous help?

What about if you're planning a wedding, for example, and you want a certain venue, but your partner likes a different one? You can't get them to change their mind and it doesn't make a difference at the end of the day, so you might "accidentally" cancel the reservation and then let your partner know that they double-booked by mistake, so now you have to look for a new venue. "Oh, look, the one you like is open for bookings! How convenient!"

Manipulation as a social tool is pretty much harmless to everyone else around you, but it brings you advantages, so it's a win-win. You get what you want, everyone else is none the wiser, and no one misses out on anything or suffers any kind of damage. What's the harm?

Take the Power in Every Relationship

The person who has control has the power, and the person who knows how to manipulate people and situations has the control. It might not seem like it's important to have the "power" in your relationships, because we like to think that our relationships are equal. But they are far from equal, and there is always one person who has more influence over the other one, a person who is in control.

When it comes to romantic relationships, traditionally, it was the man who had the power, but as society evolves and becomes more equal, so do relationships. We now like to believe that a romantic relationship can be equal, whether the partners are a man and a woman, two men, or two women. The truth is that someone is always in charge and it's not even a gender thing; it's a human thing.

Think of all the relationships in your life—your significant other, your best friend, your co-workers, etc. Isn't there always a person who gives more than the other one, while the other person is more passive? Aren't there always people who make you work harder for their love, companionship, or appreciation? A person who is more convincing than others and who somehow always manages to get everyone else to see things their way?

Congratulations, you've discovered how inter-personal relationships work. Now, think—wouldn't you want to be that person who is in charge? The person who gets their way and doesn't have to compromise? Don't get me wrong, compromise can be great and noble, but to get there, you must go through a lot of conflict, disagreement, and just straight-up fighting. Why fight over what color to paint the living room when you can just convince your significant other that your way is better? Isn't that healthier?

Or think about relationships where control is dictated by seniority, because that is what society follows. We all know its nonsense to follow someone's lead just because they're older. Respect is earned, not owed.

b) Techniques for Mind Control

Persuasion

Persuasion is the very first step on the scale of influencing behavior. Mostly harmless and decently easy to learn, persuasion is achieved through your own God-given charm and convincing abilities. Or, alternatively, that's something you can learn. Yes, that's right, if you're not very convincing, naturally, you can change that, my friend.

But what is persuasion?

Persuasion is the art of convincing. You know, attracting someone to the dark side. As far as influencing other people's behavior goes, this sits low on the list of immoral behavior or intentions. Everyone has the right to try to convince someone else of something; some of us are more effective than others, but that shouldn't be held against us.

Contrary to popular belief, persuasion isn't just spoken—when it comes to convincing someone, it's a concentrated and purposeful effort involving various elements of your being. From your posture, to your body language, to your tone of voice, and how well you maintain eye contact, it all contributes to creating the impression of confidence and influence.

That's the trick behind persuasion, in its most simple form—giving off a supremely confident vibe and creating the impression that you know exactly what you're doing. People are intimidated, impressed and charmed by confident people. They trust them, because of their own insecurities. You don't know what you're doing, but that fella over there seems to know, so let's listen to him.

Like I said, if you're not a persuasive person, you can become one. There are some tips and tricks you can employ in order to make yourself seem a different person, a better person, a more confident and persuasive person that can influence people and get what they want.

Be Mindful of Your Posture

You wouldn't believe how much our posture influences other people's opinion of us and what we represent. Think about it—who seems more confident, a person who stands up straight or a person who slouches? Who seems healthier? Who seems more successful? We believe in people we admire and people we want to emulate, so you've got to work on that posture. Keep your back straight, your shoulders back, and your head held high. Look straight ahead.

Always maintain this posture—while standing, walking, sitting, etc. This will make it easier for it to become habit. So, the next time you need to stand in front of a room full of people and be convincing, you will command respect and attention.

Your Tone Is Important

The most important lesson of all, when it comes to this part, is that your tone should fit your message. It's common sense, really—don't laugh or sound chipper if you're talking about something serious, and don't be somber if you want to tell a joke. But people often miss the mark on this one, so it's worth mentioning.

An appropriate tone will underscore your message nicely and make it sound more genuine and believable. Say it like you mean it and you will have the target in the palm of your hand.

What Kind of Energy Are You Putting Out?

What we call energy is your overall demeanor. You might not even be aware that this is a thing or that it counts, but it's one of the most important aspects of persuasion. You need to "read" your target and see what energy they are putting out. What mood are they in? Are they talkative? Do they seem tired? Cranky? Excited?

This is important to note because your energy must match theirs, otherwise, this whole show you're putting on is in vain. If you're overexcited when they're tired, that will be exhausting for them and they won't pay attention. If you're happy when they're miserable, they will be annoyed. If you're somber when they're cheery, they'll be bored. Remember that you want to retain their attention.

The Right Amount of Eye Contact

Eye contact is overwhelmingly important to the way you are perceived and how persuasive you are. But finding the right amount of eye contact is a delicate balance. Too much, and you will be perceived to be aggressive, which will put them on the defensive. Too little, and you will be perceived as not persuasive enough, so they will stop listening.

The secret is to maintain eye contact all throughout your speech, but sporadically. Look into their eyes at key moments when you're talking, in order to underline the importance of your words and make them pay closer attention. This will make you seem sincere and open. After all, if you were lying, you would be avoiding their gaze, right?

Body Language Is Half the Battle

It always comes back to body language, doesn't it? Body language can make or break your persuasiveness, so never underestimate its contribution. In order to be convincing, you must be aware of the body language you are expressing and make sure it's in line with what you're saying.

Old, stand-by advice dictates that you should keep your pose open—turn your body towards your audience, don't keep your arms crossed, keep your palms facing upward, etc. in order to put your audience at ease and express sincerity.

You should also remember not to play with your hair, drum your fingers, or fidget, because that portrays nervousness and it's not what you want to project. Self-assured body language is essential.

Build Confidence

Confidence is the common denominator here and the aspect that is most noticeable in your interactions. Everything about you must exude confidence, but that's difficult, when you don't have it. But here is how you can build it up:

Think of your failures as teachable moments — learn from them, instead of being discouraged. Now you know something new and next time you know you will do better.

Repeat a confident mantra every day — as you will later learn from this book (spoiler!), if you repeat something enough times, you start to believe it. Tell yourself "I am persuasive and great at what I do!" every day.

Put yourself in unfamiliar situations — after you do something that terrifies you, it stops being intimidating. So, embrace the opportunity for unfamiliar situations; handling them successfully will give you confidence.

What Are Some Examples of Persuasion?

A good sales pitch—Have you ever had someone try to sell you something—maybe some sort of cleaning product for your car, maybe insurance, or maybe windows for your home—and fell for it?

I can picture him now: nice dark suit, straight tie, slick hair, and a million-dollar smile. He approaches you and asks if he can have a minute of your time. You can waste a minute, so why not?

So, he starts talking about this amazing new product and how good it is. It has all these amazing features; he uses it himself and he's super happy with how it works. He even gives you a super convincing demonstration.

By the end of the sales pitch, you're left there thinking "Why not?" The guy seems passionate, confident in what he's saying, and honest. You really think that he wants the best for you, and the best is this new product. So, you hand him the money, no questions asked.

A successful presentation at work — Your co-worker is giving a presentation today. You hate presentations, because your palms get sweaty, you start stammering, and you can't stop thinking about all these people who are staring at you and judging you. Suffice it to say, your presentations aren't successful.

Your co-worker, however, glides over to the front of the room, and in the most unwrinkled skirt you've ever seen, starts confidently talking about her project. Her tone is firm, but measured, her back is straight, and her gestures all seem very intentional.

Every word she says adds to the effect of her presentation, and she never hesitates or misses a beat. She somehow manages to maintain eye contact with every single person in the room, so that you all feel like she is talking to you, personally.

She is completely relaxed, talks like she knows exactly what she's saying and why, and smiles like she doesn't have a care in the world. The result? No one dares to even question her. You all buy whatever it is she is selling without stopping to think if what she's been saying makes sense or not—she said it so well that it doesn't matter anymore.

Mind Control

Mind control, here is where it gets serious. You don't play around with mind control, it's an activity not many people engage in, and with good reason. Mind control is, perhaps, the ultimate form of persuasion, but it's more than that. It's not just your mad persuasive abilities that allow you to effectively control someone's mind. Mind control relies on tricks of psychology and next-level manipulation. Do not try this at home, kids.

What Is Mind Control?

In the simplest terms possible, mind control is the act of controlling someone else's mind. This is possible through a high level of influence, so you should know this is for advanced users, so to speak. If you're just starting out trying to influence people, you can't move straight into mind control, because you will fail, and it might become obvious what you're trying to do. That can be dangerous and can have serious social repercussions, so I would be very careful if I were you.

Now, mind control is nowhere near as dramatic as it sounds and as movies try to make it look. There is no device that will allow you to, physically control someone else's mind and mold it into whatever you want. No, actual, real life mind control is much more subtle, and it involves some very skilled and carefully calculated persuasion techniques.

It's also good to know that a lot of these high-skill, high-level powerful techniques take time to achieve, so we're playing the long-con, here. You certainly can put thoughts into people's heads and subtly exert control over what they think or do, but that takes practice, perseverance, consistency, and time. You don't want to rush a process like this, because then your plan will not develop the way it should, and your target will not assimilate the message properly.

Another point I want to make is about subtlety—always, always make sure you are not obvious in your attempts at mind control. Otherwise it will backfire in ways you have yet to understand.

What Are Some Examples of Mind Control?

Putting ideas into someone's head—Let's say you really want someone to do a certain thing. Imagine you're 12 and you want your mom to buy you the new cool pair of sneakers, or maybe you want to go to a certain vacation destination with your partner. You know that if you suggest it, they will be against the idea, so you can't outright tell them. The idea must be their own. Or it must appear that way.

This means you can't mention anything about this to them, because then they will know what you're up to. Don't address it directly, but instead, make sure they encounter the idea time and time again, but indirectly. You can achieve that through all sorts of means, the only thing you really need is creativity, persistence, and patience.

One tactic that I personally love is taking advantage of technology. You know how Google displays targeted ads that are based on your personal searches and interests? Well, it's time to screw with that algorithm and give Google a new idea to plant into your victim's head.

Suppose your birthday is coming up and you want a certain expensive watch. You can't ask for it and there is no way your partner will think about it on their own, so you have to offer a little help. Go on their computer and start searching for that watch. Do it every day, every time you find the computer unattended.

Make sure to go on specific gift websites so they'll receive the images of the watch in the context of gift-giving. Remember to delete the search history so that they won't know you looked for it. Soon, they will start receiving ads for that watch every day and they will be constantly exposed to that image. It will plant the seed in their head.

Another good idea is to sign them up for a newsletter from a store that sells the watch. These things tend to send emails every week, sometimes with discount codes and sales attached. Something like this can push your significant other over the edge, if they'd been toying with the idea of purchasing that watch for you. Or at the very least, it can get them to think about it even more than they already did.

Another trick you can employ is to co-opt a friend (or several) and have them talk about how great this watch is and how affordable it is. It's all about reinforcing the idea that's already in their head, and through these numerous and repetitive suggestions, leading them to the conclusion that they thought of the idea themselves.

Thinking for someone — If there is one thing people have in common, it's our complete and utter laziness. Believe it or not, people are even too lazy to think. It sounds ridiculous, but when you think about it, it's not that surprising, really. Our brains go into overdrive thinking about a hundred different things, every second of the day. The basic things like food, shelter, safety, etc. are a given, but civilization and social development have added worries like work stress, class anxieties, social conflicts, etc.

Ironically, the more developed we are as a species, the more work and stress we seem to add into our lives. It's no wonder mindless tasks and hobbies have gained so much popularity in recent years (adult coloring books, minimalism, Netflix, etc.); at the end of the day, we all just want to get home and not think. But with all our modern responsibilities and worries, that is unfortunately an unattainable dream, most of the time.

Keeping that in mind, when someone comes along and offers to essentially think for you, most people will jump at the chance to enjoy some rest and let someone else do the hard work, even if just for a moment.

If you're versed in manipulation, you will recognize this as an excellent opportunity to impose your own point of view. When people already have their minds made up about something, or when you ask them to think, you won't have much success. If you present them with an idea you've already thought of, on the other hand...the results are drastically different.

This is valuable advice for any area or aspect of your life, not necessarily if you want to manipulate someone. For example, you are much more likely to get someone to meet with you if you give them a specific date and time. "Hey, do you want to meet? What time would be better for you?" seems to be polite and accommodating, but ironically, it will yield poor results. If, on the other hand, you give a firm "I can meet on Tuesday at 3," you are more likely to receive an affirmative answer.

Why? First, because you allow minimal waffling. They have no room to hem and haw and change their minds and they can't put you off. Second, it's because you present a solid moment in time, that you've already thought of. All they must do is show up. No thinking. No planning. No scheduling. No worrying. Just going with whatever, you came up with. It's the easiest choice in the world to make and that's all you must do to get what you want: be the one to make the choices.

Repetition — When you repeat something several times, you remember it; that's how learning works, through practice. The same concept can be applied to mind control: latch onto an idea and repeat it to your target enough times, in different and subtle ways, and you will notice that they begin to assimilate it, only they don't know where they heart it or how they were introduced to it. They just know it's there, now.

This can be used for several things, from acquiring a skill—practice makes perfect!—to learning a language, studying, etc. Of course, repetition is an important tool in manipulation, because it's very easy to strongly suggest something to your target and have them assimilate the message. Of course, this won't work as well if it's an idea that the target does not agree with—hence why we still have political contradictions in the world.

This can be a very effective technique, but you've got to be careful about how you bring the message into discussion—if you insist too much on your idea, the target might catch on and your repetition might put the person off. If you have too much of a good thing, there's a pretty high chance that you will never want to see it or hear about it again, so you have to maintain a careful and calculated balance in order to not fall into this trap.

My suggestion is to start slowly and introduce the idea subtly. You shouldn't appear to be very eager or too set in your opinion, because that might put the target on the offensive and they will be resistant to your message. You need to display a relaxed, confident air, that puts the target at ease and makes them more likely to listen to you and open to having their opinion challenged or changed. Try to introduce the topic each time as if it's not a big deal and you just happen to be talking about it.

Chapter 9. Manipulation Rules/Techniques

Manipulators devalue every victim. They purposefully want to make others feel worthless so that they can make them bend to their will. Their never-ending mind games are damaging, to say the least. They leave their victims traumatized by the emotional pain that never seems to end. They end up mentally crippled, and they never quite understand what happened or how they can get out of it.

While many of the narcissist's tactics look like other manipulative tactics, the degree in which they happen is bigger for the narcissist. They perform manipulative acts more often than a regular manipulative person, and their literal wellbeing relies on being able to control another person. Let's look at a narcissist's favorite manipulation tactics.

They Project and Deflect

To a narcissist, they are flawless. That means if work has upset them, or if somebody has made them aware of a flaw, you are going to be who they take it out on. The worst part is that you won't have time to prepare. When you trigger them, and it can literally just be saying anything to them, you turn into the target of their aggression. This wreaks havoc on your emotional and mental health, but it can hurt your physical health as well.

They Control EVERYTHING

The bills, the social outings, the meals, the conversation, everything must be the way they want it. They must control everything so that they remain at the center of attention and are the focus of the relationship. You can try to talk about your day, but they aren't going to hear a single word you've said. If you ask them about it, they won't remember any of it.

This will eventually cause you to forget about your life and what you want. If the relationship reaches this strong of a manipulative role, stop, and figure out what is going on and see where you can go so that you can have a better quality of life.

They Gaslight

Every single manipulative tactic can cause damage to your emotional and mental health, and this because it causes you to doubt yourself and your sanity. You start questioning if you said something, or if you "forgot" to say something, or if you're the only person that sees something a certain way. This is what gaslighting does, and it works amazingly well for the narcissist because you don't have proof.

You can't prove the way you are feeling, and you can't if they have said something wrong or acted out in an irrational manner. You could record everything, but then you would be the one acting crazy. All they want to do is make sure that you must rely on them for your worth, sanity, and the basis of your reality.

They Are Forever the Victim

You are truly the one being victimized, but the narcissist always finds a way to turn things around so that they look like the victim. You may mention how it seems like you are talking to a brick wall whenever you try to tell them something, and then they will turn around and respond with, "See? I never seem to get through to you."

It never makes any sense, but you will start to question if you are the one to blame. Maybe you weren't clear. Don't let yourself fall for this manipulation.

They Minimize Your Worth

When you started your relationship with the narcissist, they complimented everything you did and made you feel as if you two would be the best couple in the world. You were happy, but then things changed. The compliments became suggestions of what you should do to make yourself better. How you fixed your hair was silly or childish. Your puns that all of your friends like.

"Those are dumb. They only laugh because they feel sorry for you." You will get to a point where you will only feel as worthy as what they say you are.

They Bring in Reinforcements

The narcissist must have back up. They have huge egos, and they are as fragile as they big. This means that no matter what you say, how logical you are being, or what facts you have, you are never going to win. It's impossible. They have already managed to trick their colleagues and friends into taking their side.

You don't know this, though. Now you must face a conversation the narcissist and a third-party member that they have picked out. This is a recipe for disaster.

They Shame in Public and Private

The narcissist will always make belittling comments to you no matter where you are. They feed off making you feel small, appear less intelligent, or look weak. This is a very subtle and extremely dangerous tactic. It gets disguised as, "I'm only kidding." Eventually, you start to need those hurtful remarks, or you hope that one day you finally become good enough and they won't say those hurtful things anymore.

Trust me, you are good enough now.

They Target Insecurities and Flaws

The narcissist has an amazing ability to find out a person's insecurities and to discover everything that the person sees as a flaw. They remember every piece of this information and they perfectly time when they are going to use this against their victim.

They might bluntly ask about these things, using intimacy and vulnerability as a cover to help remove any defense that they may find. The victim thinks they are building and strengthening their bond, but the narcissist sees it to store up some ammunition for an attack.

When the time is right, they will attack. They use the information that you provided to reopen old wounds, which causes you to relive the trauma and pain you have worked hard to overcome. They thrive on this power that they have over you, and they will use it whenever they need.

They Use Their Tone, Volume, and Silence

Sometimes, a narcissist most powerful approach is the silent approach. When in a confrontation, they may simply choose to turn away, shake their head, frown, or glare at you.

If they don't go silent, they could change the volume of their voice to change how their message comes across. They could get quieter or louder. Either one is showing the evilness bubbling under the surface. They can also change up their tone in order to convey a different message. They may speak higher when on the defensive or emphasize certain words to help push their own agenda.

All these manipulation tactics are meant to exert control and influence over their victim. A narcissist will take whichever approach they need to in order to get their way. They wear their victim down with their non-stop approach. Identifying these things is the first step in getting your life back.

Chapter 10. Understand Manipulation Techniques and Act Accordingly

Every person you talk to will have their own perception of things. You can get five people to watch the same thing happen, and they will all describe it in a different way. What you personally believe is wrong, could be the right thing for someone else. It is how the mind works, and there is not much that you will be able to do about it. Sometimes though, when you get frustrated with someone who does not seem to understand what you want from them, or when you can't figure out why someone you are close to is acting differently, then you may want to know exactly why people do the things they do.

It is important to realize that people have their own minds. Everyone is different, and you are not going to find two people who are exactly alike. Even when you run into twins, you will find that they will have very different views on the world and different personalities. There are many reasons why people may be different. It could be things like their culture, their gender, their environment, their thoughts, feelings, habits, emotions, and more.

We All Have Different Motivations

You will find that there is an unwritten rule in actions and behaviors, and that is that all people will act based on the things that motivate them. People will act and do things in a different way because there are differences in what they need and want. Each person may choose to use different strategies to attain these needs and wants.

Now, there is no right or wrong answer here, mainly because most people will have their own concept of what is right for them. It is all about the perception. People do have the same core needs, which means that while personalities might change on the surface, everyone starts out in the same boat. It is also possible that there will be more than one of these basic human needs that can motivate you, which means there are many reasons for the actions that you complete. Each person may have similar core needs, but we can still have varying degrees of awareness when it comes to the relationship between our actions and our needs.

When you are not aware of the things that you need, you may start actions based on your feelings, your impulses, habits, and thoughts. Each of these types of motivation can be a reason to take responsibility for the choices that you make. Everything that you do will connect back to your needs, and you will continue with this without thinking about what you are doing.

Our Thoughts and Feelings

There are many times when we will do things simply because we feel that we had to do them. In addition, we may do things because our emotions, such as satisfaction, joy, and happiness will lead us to do things because we want to feel these emotions. In addition, there are times when we will want to avoid certain things because we want to avoid some of the negative feelings, such as shame, guilt, and fear.

Feelings, in humans, are immediately going to be translated into action, and often this will happen without truly understanding what is wanted. Most of the time, the feelings will give a more commanding action so that you will just act rather than first thinking about and trying to understand the action that is behind it. So, if someone can play on your emotions, such as working on your fear or your need to be liked and wanted, they are more likely to get you to act the way that they want, even if you do not fully understand why you are acting that way.

Understanding the Brain

Our brains are complex. We have two parts that come together to make us who we are. We have the more complex parts that may be newer among mammals but allow us to have rational thoughts. But then we have the limbic system that forms the emotions and how we should react to the things that are going on around us. Both helps to make us modern humans, but they are sometimes going to make us react in ways that we do not fully understand.

Essentially, to build up the emotional intelligence (EQ) that we need, we must have effective communication between the rational brain and the older and more primitive emotional structures that come with the limbic system. This is known as neuroplasticity, and it is basically the process of forming new neural pathways in the brain in response to learning new things.

You can use a variety of strategies to develop your own EQ levels in the same way. When you use these strategies, you are working to strengthen the billions of neuron pathways that are found in the brain. This will also allow those pathways to branch out and form connections with the cells that are nearby, which will improve your cognitive ability.

As this process continues to expand, it will essentially increase the rate of positive feedback loops and will ensure that anything that you practice on a regular basis will be habitual in nature, making it easier to perform in the future.

As you can imagine by this, there will be a large separation between the thinker and the feeler in each person, and both can pull you in different directions. This is what will leave many people open to manipulative behavior, especially if the thinker and the feeler inside are not aligned properly.

Your feelings are the things that will compel you to do things from within, while your thoughts will compel you to do things from without. This is an important thing to remember because it can show the freedom of being able to choose rather than being compelled to do something.

When it comes to making a choice, that choice is always going to be internal. The individual will be able to decide whether they will do something or not. For most individuals, they will take into consideration what consequences will occur from their actions before they make any decisions. There is a difference between believing that you need to do something, and choosing things based on what is important.

So, you will see that your thoughts will contain a variety of information about many things that you hold important and can be an expression of your needs. There are those who do not have a vibrancy of feeling. Those who are better able to manage their feelings are simply those who have more control over these feelings.

How Can a Manipulator Step in?

At this point, you may be wondering how the manipulator can step in and use this to their advantage. Remember we talked about how when you learn a new skill, your neurons can form new paths that get stronger the more that you practice? This skill can be anything from learning how to bake something for dinner to learning how to behave in church.

The manipulator will use this to their advantage. They will slowly be able to teach you the way that you should behave. They may suggest a certain course of action, and if you do not follow it, they will start to do actions that will train your brain to behave the way that they want, and they will utilize your emotions to help make that connection stronger than ever.

Let us say the manipulator does not want you going out with friends at night because they want you to instead hang out with them and make dinner. You may fight this a few times and say you want to go out and see friends anyway. They can then resort to the fear emotion, yelling at you and demeaning you. Any time that you decide you want to go out with friends, they will start up with the yelling and fighting. Any time that you agree to stay home, they will pick another emotion, such as love. Your brain will quickly catch on to this pattern, and you are more likely to do what the manipulator wants to avoid the fear and receive the love.

This is just one example of how a manipulator can use the workings of the brain against you. They are usually able to do it in such a covert way, and over enough time, that it becomes hard for the target to know what is going on or how to make it all stop.

Chapter 11. Manipulation and Moral Question: Why Is Manipulation Important in Life

There are going to be certain times in your life when you will find that manipulation is going to come in handy. While you know that it is so important to practice in as many scenarios as you can, there are going to be ones that you will find manipulation will be the most useful. In this chapter, we are going to focus on the best places where you can use the skills of manipulation so that you can get ahead and really benefit from the things that you have learned so far.

Business Negotiations

When it comes to working on some negotiations in business, it is easy to see how you want to make sure that you can get your way. Getting your own way will usually mean that you want to close a better deal, one that is going to be highly favorable to your own company. Closing these deals, and making sure that they are in your favor, will mean that your company is able to get most, if not all, of the things that it is asking for, and that you will barely have to deal with any inconveniences in the process to do this.

There are a lot of things that you can negotiate during these meetings, such as better terms on the deals, better pricing on the services, and more, and if you use your skills in manipulation, you are more likely to get the whole thing to work in your favor.

When it comes to negotiating on some better deals for the business, you will find that manipulation is a very powerful tool for you to use. Whether others like to admit to this or not, negotiations are rarely fair, and there is usually going to be a person who comes out on top. You want to make sure that the person who comes out on top is you.

When you use manipulation in these efforts, it means that you are easily able to dominate the conversation, without the other person even realizing it. When this happens, others in the negotiation are more likely to give in without even doing a fight, because they think they are getting something good out of it as well. Because of this, and all the good benefits that you can get from this, you should bring out the manipulation skills that you learn as much as possible when you are working with a business negotiation.

Closing Sales

If you are at all involved in a sales process at some point, then you know that it is not always easy to close sales. If you work in retail, for example, you likely notice that many of the people who come into your store are dreaming and looking around, and sometimes, they won't be prepared to buy anything. Because of this, it can sometimes be valuable to know how to manipulate people as you can encourage them to spend money that they did not otherwise intend to spend.

What this means is that when you get the other person to purchase something through your manipulation techniques, it results in more sales for the business. If you are the one who owns the company, you know how important this is. If you are an employee, you know that effective numbers of sales, and good sales strategies, means that you are more likely to be respected by your employer, and then you can make it up the ladder of the company.

If you are in a sales position that is considered business to business, then you know that manipulation is so important. People who end up going to a meeting with you are likely interested in what you are going to offer, but they could also be shopping around to a few different companies at the same time, and you need to find ways that will put your business ahead of all the other choices that they are considering.

Knowing how to use the right skills of manipulation at any level of sales means that they can close more deals and that they will be left with happier customers. This only means that good things are going to be available for you in the future.

Getting Prices That Are Better

You can use manipulation from the other side of the perspective as well. If you are the customer and knowing how to manipulate during this time can be highly valuable. As you know, many times the salespeople have been given some room to negotiate with their customers in order to encourage sales. This means that if you are willing to use some manipulation and work with them, you can get a special and better deal. You are able just to take the price, but wouldn't it be much better for you to go through and get a better price if you are able to.

Being effective at manipulation means that you can easily manipulate companies to give you the best in deals for services and products. By promising them your praise and services, for example, you can essentially get them in the palm of your hand. They become far more willing to communicate with their managers and negotiate the best possible deal for you so that you will actively buy from them. Salespeople, especially those who are based on commission, are always eager to close a deal. This allows you to use manipulation in order to get the deal to close in your favor.

Leading the Desired Lifestyle That You Want

Each person has a goal about the desired lifestyle that they would like to have—but the lifestyle that you have right now, and the one that you desire, might not always be the same thing. However, the good thing about using manipulation is that you can use it to help you get to the desired lifestyle. There are a lot of ways that you can do this—you just need to learn how to make it work.

Let's say that right now you are living in a house that you are renting, and you want to buy your own home at some point—but right now, the types of homes that you are the most interested in purchasing are not within the price that you can purchase. However, with the right kind of manipulation, you may find that you are able to get a better deal, putting you into the home of your dreams sooner as you would like. This can work with any of the big-ticket items that you would like to purchase, such as cars.

Another way that this can work is with some of the relationships that you are in. If you are someone who would like to find a new group of friends, the friends who are going to help you reflect your new lifestyle, you may find that working with manipulation is going to help you out. You can also use the art of persuasion to convince others to become your friends and spend time with you—and from that, you will then have the friends that you need to live this new lifestyle.

Take this a step further and see how it can work with some of your intimate relationships. If this kind of relationship doesn't look like the one that you would like, then you can bring in some manipulation and see if it is possible to make the right changes towards a better relationship. If you want to have more romance, for example, you will spend some time with fancier places or people.

Getting Out of Things

Have you ever gotten into a situation where you were asked to do something, but you didn't have any want to do it? All the time we are going to be signed up for things, or given offers, that we aren't really that interested in—and sometimes, it can feel difficult to turn these things down in a polite manner. Depending on who is asking for the favor, you may feel obligated to help them out with it.

However, once you learn how to work with manipulation a bit more, you will find that this is not as big of a problem for you anymore. You may even find that this is a good place to start when it comes to practicing your manipulation. You can bring it up any time that you get stuck doing something that you would rather not be doing.

Not only are you able to use manipulation for your benefit to get out of the reunions or things that family and friends want you to help with, but you can also use it at work as well. If your boss went and signed you up for something that you don't want to do, you can use manipulation to convince them to let you get out of it, or you can convince someone else to go and do the work for you.

You can use manipulation in any manner that you would like to make sure that you are able to live the life that you want. It can help you to get the business negotiations to work the way that you want, to help you get the friendships, relationships, and to get yourself out of the things that you don't want to do. There are just so many different things that you can use manipulation with, and this can be a great way to ensure that you have the life that you have always dreamed about.

Work on Self-Esteem to Overcome Manipulation

To overcome manipulation you have to examine your inner self. There is something about you that makes manipulators believe they can have easy control over you. Here's an example.

Stacy has learned since childhood that expressing emotions is a good thing. People will appreciate you more when they understand you, and if a person can't express their emotions, they will live a lonely life. This way how Stacy was psychologically conditions during her childhood, but as she got older, her personality becomes too vulnerable.

Stacy is now a very skilled advertiser, but her lack of confidence keeps you from being recognized. She hasn't developed confidence. Instead, she is emotionally vulnerable when she doesn't need to be. She apologizes for everything, and she worries if she is liked by others. In fact, she has even asked her colleagues whether they like her. This is causing her to lose friends, which is the opposite of what her parents made her believe.

Some emotional vulnerability is great in relationships, but if you let it go too far, it leaves you open to manipulators. You must also have self-confidence or self-esteem. Having both emotional vulnerability and self-esteem will help you to know when it is safe to be vulnerable and when you need to stick up for yourself. This makes it a lot harder for the manipulator to take control.

Self-esteem is the way in which you perceive and value yourself. It is your own beliefs and opinions about yourself, which are likely going to be hard to change because you have had them for so long. Your self-esteem can affect:

- If you value and like yourself

- If you can make decisions for yourself and assert them

- If you can see your positives and strengths

- If you are willing to try new things

- If you can show yourself kindness

- If you can move on from mistakes without unfairly blaming yourself

- If you take personal time

- If you believe that you are good enough
- If you believe that you deserve to be happy

There are many different things that can cause low self-esteem. Your self-esteem could end up changing suddenly, or you could have always suffered from low self-esteem. Either way, it can be hard to notice that you have low self-esteem and make it hard to change it. The following things can create low self-esteem:

- Housing or money problems
- Body image worries
- Divorce, separation, or other relationship problems
- Mental health problems
- Physical health problems
- Ongoing stress
- Problems with school or work
- Having a hard time find a job or losing your job
- Experiencing a stigma, discrimination, or prejudice
- Being abused or bullied

It doesn't matter what caused low self-esteem. A manipulator can use your low self-esteem to gain control over you.

Let's look at how you can improve your self-esteem to avoid manipulation.

Be Mindful

There's no way of changing something if you can't spot it and know it needs to be changed. Simply becoming aware of how you talk to yourself will start to pull you away from the negativity. You want to stop self-limiting talk. When you notice yourself falling down the rabbit hole of self-criticism or doubt, take note of what is happening, and then tell yourself, "These are only thoughts and not the truth."

Change Your Story

Everybody has a story they have created about their self. This story shapes our perceptions, which is what your self-image is based upon. In order to change it, you must know where it originated. Whose voices have you internalized?

Most negative thoughts that have become automatic were learned from somebody else, and that means you can unlearn them. What is it that you want to believe about yourself? Start repeating those things in your mind and your story will start to change.

Stop Comparing

Accept who you are and stop comparing yourself to other people. Just because one of your friends seems super happy in their Facebook posts doesn't mean they truly are. Comparing yourself will only cause negative self-talk, which lowers your self-esteem. You are enough as you are.

Channel Your Strengths

Everybody has their own strengths and weaknesses. You could be an amazing chef but lousy at singing. These things don't define your worth. Recognize your strength and the confidence that they bring you, especially if you are feeling down. When something doesn't go right, remind yourself of all the ways in which you rock.

You Are Not Your Circumstances

You must learn to differentiate yourself from your circumstances. Know your inner worth and love your imperfect self. This will provide you with a foundation to grow. This will pull you away from the fear of failure and allow you to grow unencumbered.

Accept Compliments

One of the hardest things about improving your self-esteem is that when you feel bad about yourself, it is a lot hard to accept compliments even though they are exactly what you need. Work on tolerating compliments whenever one is given to you, even if you are completely uncomfortable. One of the best ways to avoid responding in a negative way is to have set responses to compliments and then train yourself to say them when you receive good feedback. You can say things like "That was nice of you to say," and "Thank you."

Everybody has infinite potential and equal worth. The stronger your self-esteem is, the harder it will be for a manipulator to grab hold of you.

Chapter 12. Psychological Manipulation Through Words

When people don't answer you, when they use sarcasm, telling you it's impossible to talk to you, threatening you with ultimatums, or talking to you like you were a child, these signs of psychological manipulation through language and communication are exhausting. This is a form of emotional abuse and mental exploitation that we must learn to recognize.

One of the most sinister men in Italian history was Licio Gelli. He was an agent of the Masonic Lodge Propaganda Due. He was a neo-fascist who specialized in manipulating masses. This evil person once said that to control anyone, you had to know how to communicate. He showed us that language can be used as a weapon and can be used to dominate.

Many people know this too well. Within the realm of politics, in media, in advertising there is constant use of manipulation to control us, influence our decisions, and yes, to seduce us. Once we come into our private realm, everything gets a bit more complex and mantic.

We are talking about the way we communicate with our friends, significant other, family, etc. If you just stop and look, you can see signs of emotional and psychological manipulation all around you, but these are usually camouflaged. You might also fall into a trap of using it yourselves. You must know how to detect it and how to react to it.

You must know that it isn't just important to watch what you say but how you say it.

Signs of Psychological Manipulation

When we talk about psychological manipulation by using words, what happens first will be an imbalance in a relationship. It is using language to benefit yourself. Not to just control a person but to harm them as well. Bare emotions are what cause this aggression in you.

Aldous Huxley once said that words are like X-rays. If they are used in a Machiavellian way, they could pierce through everything: another person's self-esteem, their identity, and dignity. You must learn to see them coming, to know a bit more about this personally. Here are some warning signs:

Manipulating Facts

Anyone who is an expert in manipulating through communication is a strategist who is great at twisting the truth. They will always turn everything around to their favor, lower their share of responsibility, and blame anyone but themselves. They will also withhold and exaggerate important information to make sure the balance will always tilt toward their "truth."

They Say You Are Impossible to Talk to

This approach is effective, direct, and very simple. If anyone tells you that "you are impossible to talk to," they are avoiding exactly what you are wanting to do: talking about the problem. It's common for them to say you are too emotional, you are "making a mountain out of a molehill," and they can't talk with you. They will accuse you of what they have problems with, and this is poor communication skills.

Harassing Intellectually

An emotional and psychological manipulator uses another common strategy: intellectual harassment. They will constantly throw arguments your way. They will also make sure the information is different and the facts are so twisted just trying to emotionally exhaust you and convince you that they are correct.

Ultimatums With No Time to Decide

You might have heard someone say: "If you can't accept what I am saying, then it's all over." They might have gone one further with you have until tomorrow to think about it. This communication style is very distressing and painful. They have put you between a rock and a hard place and generate a lot of emotional suffering along with anxiety.

You must know that if somebody respects you, and truly loves you, they will never use "all or nothing" threats. This is just one more manipulation strategy.

Constantly Saying Your Name While Talking

If somebody constantly says your name during a heated conversation, they are using a control mechanism. When they do this, they are forcing you to pay attention and causing you to feel intimidated.

Black Humor and Irony

If they like using black humor and irony, they are trying to ridicule and humiliate you. This is another sign of psychological manipulation in communication. They are trying to belittle you and trying to impose their superiority on you.

Using Evasiveness or Silence

If they say things like: "Now isn't a good time," "I don't want to talk about it," "Why are you bringing that up now?" All of this is common with significant others, especially if one doesn't have a good sense of responsibility or communication skills.

Claiming Ignorance

If somebody says to you: "I don't understand what you mean," this is another tactic. They will pretend not to understand what you are wanting them to do or say. They are playing mind games. They want to make it look like you are complicating things and the conversation doesn't make any sense. This is a strategy that passive-aggressive manipulators like to use to avoid taking responsibility and wants to make you suffer.

They Allow You to Talk First

The most subtle sign of psychological manipulation is when they always make you talk first. By doing this, they achieve many things. The first one is buying time to get their argument ready. The second is to figure out your weak points. It is common that after they have listened to you, they won't express their opinion or ideas. They will only ask more questions. Rather than reaching some sort of an agreement, they try to highlight your shortcomings. They will direct the conversation in ways that make you look weak and clumsy.

Yes, there are many other strategies that emotional and psychological manipulator could use when communicating but the above are the most common. These try to intimidate you and keep you from establishing effective dialogues, but they try to subdue you. They are trying to incapacitate you on all levels: mentally, emotionally, and personally. You must learn how to see these destructive strategies.

Silent Treatment = Emotional Abuse

What does "silent treatment" mean? It is refusing to verbally engage with another person, often because of a conflict within the relationship. Some refer to it as stonewalling or the cold shoulder. It is used as a passive-aggressive way to control others. It can be considered emotional abuse. If you think it is normal for your significant other to go for days without speaking to you, think again. Silence can be used productively like right after a breakup or if you are taking a time to cool off but prolonged times of unresponsiveness in relationships aren't healthy or normal.

At times, you might not have anything to say. Sometimes disconnecting is a good idea so that each party can take a moment to reflect on what has happened and then come back once they have received some clarity. Arguments aren't ever pleasant, but they come and go and might leave new understanding.

Most of us have been at a place where we don't want to face the argument and it is not because we fear an escalation. We refuse to go back in because we are trying to punish them.

The silent treatment is one of the most powerful tools that a passive-aggressive manipulator could use. It keeps their opponent on edge while giving you a sense of power. It demands emotional and mental perfection from other people that don't exist in anyone. Ignoring somebody like this is very hurtful. All the emotional effects might last and frankly, this is very unfair.

Dealing with It

If you are the one that is being ignored and you want to work through it, what can you do about it?

Apologize? Grovel? They are useless because the goal of the silent treatment is to make you suffer. You don't want yourself to suffer. You also don't want your loved one to feel like they must trap you into suffering in order to have control over you.

In order to react to this treatment requires a dose of humility, understanding, openness, and sensitivity. What you can do is simple, and you don't have to "take the high road" in the situation. Stances like this are just variations of you falling right into the trap they set because you will soon get tired of trying to fix things.

What you can do is be honest, since this is what you want from them, right? You can say something like: "I would really love to figure out what is wrong," since it requires two people to have an argument.

You must be sincere, and you shouldn't pretend that you haven't noticed their silent treatment; that is simply putting gas on a fire. Acting honestly won't be easy because you will be confused. You feel hurt and guilty, which is a dangerous mix.

Creating this mixture of feelings is what the manipulator wants. They want you to be voiceless and feel horrible, which makes you feel terrible.

When you are faced with the silent treatment, it's like trying to play a game of Clue with the board flipped over and without any pieces. You want to be able to solve the problem, but this has more to do with not knowing what you have done wrong or something so tiny the silencer feels the need to control the relationship for some time.

Being the receiver of this manipulation is extremely hard. Not understanding what was done, not understanding what you should say, your feelings being disrespected and disregarded, all the doubts that are planted on if the relationship was viable, as well as the guilt of feeling you created a crack in something wonderful, is a game you will eventually lose. It doesn't do anything but drop more anger onto a volatile situation.

Getting out of this type of situation will take a lot of patience. This is what is needed if you want to continue the relationship. The silencer's cycle of allowing you to come back is just a blame game that they have thought up for you to overlook any damage that they have caused.

Simplicity

Feeling like you have fed your significant other poison and you are struggling to find a way to fix it is no way to live. Don't accept anyone's ploy for power, never internalize it, and don't accept it as being a sign that you are a failure. Understand this, you didn't do anything wrong. Having a grievance is one thing, but constantly being treated unfairly from others isn't.

If you are emotionally abusive, overbearing, or manipulative, too, there isn't anything you should do but say goodbye to each other. The silent treatment's main purpose is to wear you down.

Granted, we have heard all sorts of advice from others about love. Communication and love aren't a game of picking sides, keeping score, or winning.

There are two rules that will serve us well during our time here: "Being good to each other and being good for each other." This type of situation isn't an either, or. This is an "and" situation and you must make sure it stays that way, or you will spin out of control.

Using the silent treatment isn't a good way to satisfy these things. And no matter what anybody else has to say, the single word, Hi, can provide you with satisfaction. This hi may be awkward, and it could make you feel like you are drowning or like a restrained panther, but it must be said.

Reality is a great place to start a conversation. But silence can sometimes sound like a scream

When is Silent Treatment Right?

There is a place and time for silence. There are circumstances where silence is recommended. In toxic relationships where one person tries to resolve the conflict, but the aggression is escalated silence is acceptable. Staying quiet is a way to help you cope with the person and situation. Silence can be used to protect and to help calm down after an altercation.

Silence can also be used as a boundary if you have just removed yourself from a relationship with a sociopath or narcissist.

How to Know if Silence is Abusive

You must ask yourself: "Am I being forced to defend myself or am I the one attacking them?" This is where you will find the difference. If you remain silent just to gain an upper hand and to make them suffer, then that is abuse.

If you keep your mouth shut to avoid suffering abuse, that is self-defense. If you aren't sure, it will help to answer these next few questions:

You Are Calm Again, But You Still Expect Them yo Make the Next Move

When an argument happens, it might take time for feelings to come back down. Silence in these situations isn't bad since it can keep you doing or saying something you might regret.

If you are staying silent, act after you have calmed down since you will insist that they make the first move toward reconciliation. This is a bit abusive. If you want to talk, open a dialogue.

Will Just a Complete Apology Do?

Will you stay silent for as long as they don't give you an apology? They might have shown some remorse and are trying to make amends. It isn't what you had in mind while you are ruminating. If efforts have been made toward an apology, it is right for you to move from your position to end the treatment you have given them.

This isn't saying that you have forgiven them, but you should have a conversation about what happened and why it makes you feel like you do. When you don't engage, you are choosing to keep them back, which might be emotional abuse.

Are You Responsible For The Disagreement?

At times the other person is completely wrong. There are things that aren't excusable. This isn't always the case. If you are keeping silent despite fault falling at your feet, you are ignoring the role you had in the argument that led you to where you are. This is abusive because it puts all the blame on the other person and makes them feel bad.

Will You Keep This Up For a Certain Time Frame?

When somebody does something that annoys you, don't think that you aren't going to talk with them for the remainder of the day. This can be viewed as abusive since it is giving a sentence for the crime, no matter how you may feel at any time in the future. It is telling the other person they deserve this punishment. It doesn't leave any room for forgiveness or feelings getting better between the two of you.

Chapter 13. 9 Brilliant Strategies for Seducing A Person Using Manipulation

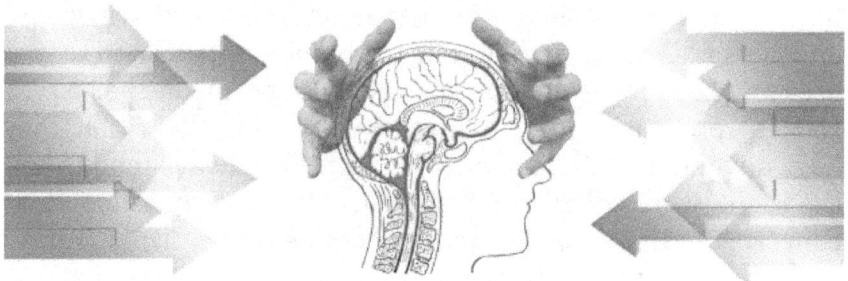

So, you're playing the seduction game and leading someone to get intimidated by you? Again, manipulation is a powerful weapon in your arsenal that can be used negatively or positively to achieve your objectives with the person, even though it may have largely negative connotations. There are plenty of psychological tricks that can be used to get close to a person or lead them to be intimate with you.

Exercise due caution and diligence when it comes to using these techniques because your dignity and reputation are at stake here. Playing with other people's emotions constantly to have your way will make you come across as distrustful, deceptive and selfish.

1. Flattery

Flattery is a brilliant way to break the ice with someone you've just met or lead someone you know for ages to do what you want. Ensure that you disguise flattery (however fake it is) in the garb of genuine and specific compliments.

For example, instead of telling someone how lovely they look in a piece of clothing, say something like, "I love how the color of your eyes is beautifully complemented by what you are wearing." It sounds more genuine and invariably draws the person to you.

There is a secret strategy when it comes to resorting to flattery. Identify an area where the person is slightly insecure and needs reassurance. Use specific compliments related to that area to win over the person. For instance, if someone has issues related to speaking confidently in public, tell them that they have a wonderful voice texture or that they always tend to use the right words while talking. This directly squashes their concerns and insecurities and makes them feel nice about an area they aren't too sure about.

2. Make Them Indebted to You

This is another slightly insidious strategy that can be used to seduce a person or get them to do what you want. It is universal strategy that is effective across cultures, classes, and genders. You make the subject feel indebted to you by doing them a series of favors. In their mind, they become obliged to you even though they didn't really ask for it.

You create a misbalanced equation where you are the giver, and they are a receiver. To make the equation more balanced, they know they must pay you back in some form. Take advantage of this titled balance and get them to do what you want by asking them in a straightforward manner when the time comes. There are high chances the person has already mentally conditioned himself or herself to pay you back. Evil as it sounds; the tactic is used by several people who will fund the lifestyles of others to make them feel indebted to the manipulator. The subtext is, "I own you because I pay for everything you use." It may start with small things that the subject voluntary opts for, which later becomes impossible to get out of.

3. Use Shame or Guilt

There's no denying that the manipulation seduction game can get sneaky and complicated with blurred lines of what is right and wrong. However, here's another technique that is widely used by the manipulator to charm people into going out or sleeping with them. It comprises inducing feelings of guilt or shame on the subject.

If the manipulator's requests are continuously turned down, he or she will be making the subject feel guilty or shameful about refusing them. For example, "You know how lonely I am, living all alone away from my family. I've had a very rough and lonely childhood where no one ever loved or cared for me. You are also adding to my feelings of being lonely and uncared for with your cold and disinterested attitude. I know the world is against me and no one wants me."

Manipulators know how to induce feelings of guilt by pushing the right emotional buttons. You will make more sweeping statements (no one loves me, the world is against me, or I've had a rough childhood) rather than state specific instances. Manipulators cleverly study what makes the other person feel guilty and target those areas to get what they want.

Another rather disturbing yet highly successful seduction manipulation technique is to make the other person feel shameful about their past actions repeatedly. Though it may help you get what you want in the short run, it will certainly not set the basis for a healthy, rewarding and meaningful relationship in future.

4. Steer the Conversation

Seducers who've mastered the art of manipulation will almost always hold the remote control of a conversation to lead their subject into doing what they want. For example, if you want to sweet talk with a date, spouse, crush or friend who is nagging you about something, you simply steer the course of the conversation by changing the topic to a more favorable one.

"Hey I just saw a gorgeous blue, low-cut outfit that would look really flattering on you at Mary Ann's boutique the other day" or "I saw the most jaw-droppingly beautiful house at Lakeview Lane on my way to work the other day, what do you think about living there together?" This takes the conversation from a rather unpleasant tone into a more welcoming and inviting tone that sets the pace for wooing someone or triggering feelings of intimacy in them.

5. False Logic

This one is mostly used by the teens and adolescents, but there's no denying that plenty of adult's resort to it too. The logical fallacy or false logic creation technique comprises creating a seemingly false argument and making it sound that it is indeed true. When you tell someone that if a thing is true, then he or she would not do something that is seen as undesirable by you.

For example, "if you really love me, you will get married to me immediately" or "if you trust me, you won't hesitate to go to bed with me" You are basically challenging them to prove their feelings and emotions by getting them to do what you want them to.

6. Make it Appear Normal

So, what you as a manipulator are doing here is making the subject feel like what you've asked for or what you want them to do is normal. To do this, you stealthily use numbers, statistics and research findings for your advantage. You make the other person feel like it is them who thinks or feels differently, while what you are asking for is normal. This way they are led into believing that something is wrong with their thinking.

For example, "statistics reveal that 75% of people end up sleeping with each other right after the first date." You are establishing that it's a norm and that most people would do it, and they are crazy or abnormal if they think otherwise.

7. Silent Treatment

Seduction experts using manipulation know how to use the silent treatment all too well. This works like magic when you're getting someone to obey your wishes. When you remain silent, it creates an impact on the other person by making them feel like they have done something wrong or hurtful.

They become even more eager to make up for it when they realize that you are hurt, angry or upset with their actions. You will have people eating out of your hands when the subject feels the need to make up for their hurtful actions.

8. The Mirror Effect

As someone who is using the mirror effect manipulation technique for seducing the subject, you are attempting to establish a level of trust and emotional comfort by convincing the other person that you are exactly like them. The manipulator pretends to have the same background, values, interests, personality traits as the subject. You may also share fake stories, secrets or confessions to build a sense of trust, familiarity and emotional proximity with the other person. You let them know what they want to hear emotionally, and they return the favor with what you them to, often sexual in nature.

This is the basis of most seduction-manipulation techniques. Manipulate someone's emotions to lead them to think and feel in a way, and then get them to go to bed with you.

9. Create a Compelling Want

Seduction is all about creating a compelling desire and then presenting yourself as the source for fulfilling it. This is pretty much what every advertiser, salesperson and internet marketer use. They create the need for a specific thing in the lives of their prospective customers and then present their products or services as the only solution for it.

Build a strong need for what you have to offer. Make them feel like they need you to fulfill their physical and emotional objectives. Do not be afraid to show them how you can help them or what you can offer them. Strut your strengths and tease until they are convinced that you've got what they need!

Maintain a little distance from the subject to show him or what they desire is slightly out of their reach. They will be yearning for you more when they realize that you have everything they want and are yet out of their reach. This makes them strive for your attention even harder!

Deal With the Manipulative Friend

First, you need to be direct. If you suspect that your friend is manipulating you, do not get dragged into a pointless charade. Give the other person a chance to explain him/her mission by asking about it without mincing words. A true friend who has your best interests at heart will be honest. On the other hand, a manipulative friend will try to rationalize his/her words to stay in control.

- Avoid playing mind games because they are just a waste of time. Again, spending too much time with a master manipulator gives him/her the chance to study you and identify ways to apply their skills.

- Be wary of someone who is not willing to share his/her true feelings, thoughts and intentions. Something is brewing.

Secondly, keep a level head. When you realize that your trusted friend has been manipulating you, there are high chances of taking things personally. It is advisable for the victim to stay calm and not take the manipulative tactics personally. It is natural to feel upset when you realize that someone has broken the trust had but blowing up only heightens issues. You will handle the situation more effectively with a maintained poise.

- A manipulator may even be looking for a way to make you angry in order to affect your reasoning ability. Do not fall for the emotional games.

- Always delay a confrontation until you have the chance to cool off.

Thirdly, learn how to say no. One of the things preventing us from saying no is the feeling of guilt. Sometimes we do not want to look bad in front of our friends, therefore, we agree with all they ask. On the other hand, a manipulator takes advantage of these feelings. Do not give in to the demands of a self-centered friend. Regardless of the level of friendship between you and your friends, there is no rule saying you must do everything they ask. If something does not add up for you, simply and firmly say no. You may give the friend your reasons for saying no but know that do not owe anyone an explanation. Once you learn to say no and have used it in enough times, you will shift the power balance towards the center.

- You are not obliged to say yes to anyone. You also do not have to offer excuses or justify your No. Simply say no and be firm in your stand. The manipulator might try to sway you and he/she succeeds, you will remain in the manipulation cycle.

- There are times when everyone needs genuine help, whether they are manipulators or not. When asked for help, take time to analyze the situation. Are you being played or is the person in question in real need?

Stick up for yourself. As noted earlier, manipulators prey on people with self-esteem issues. IT is very hard to manipulate a person with high self-esteem and confidence. Speaking up for yourself sends the message that you are not a pushover and manipulators will keep off. So long as you feel and appear confident, the manipulator will not be able to pressure you.

- If you go out of your way to accommodate the opinions of a critic companion, you show the manipulator that you are not sure of your stand, therefore, he/she can impose him/herself.

- If for instance, you have a friend who keeps ridiculing your dressing code because they look or feel better than you, respond by simply saying "I like my sense of style. It is just different from yours but still good."

Do whatever suits you best. Note that, there is a great difference between taking orders and taking advice. Some of your mates will develop the habit of meddling with your business and giving their opinions even when they are not asked. Do not feel afraid to tell them off, after all, it is your life. Some of the opinions may be put to practice and be beneficial but ensure that no one is ordering you around. At the end of the day, you have the final say in your life.

- A true friend will give you genuine advice. In fact, he/she might not like the man or woman you are dating but will never tell you to stop seeing them. Instead, your friend will point out the things he/she feel are wrong then leave you to decide.

- Spend some time identifying what is best for you. When you have clear goals, it is hard for a person to just sway you. List down your limits and goals. What are your limits? How far can you go for a friend? These questions can help you set limits in your relationships.

Tell your friend. As mentioned earlier, some manipulators are not applying their tactics consciously. Some of these manipulators think their behavior is normal. Your manipulative friend might not be aware of the consequences of his/her actions. Talking to them about their practices might help them the mistake in their ways. When a genuine friend sees the results of his/her actions, he/she will be willing to change. However, a fake friend will try to justify their behavior and keep doing the same manipulative things in future.

- When telling your friend about their behavior, make sure you do not sound like you are questioning their character.

- Remember that everyone can manipulate others from time to time, intentionally or unintentionally. Getting the issue at hand out in the open is the first step to finding a solution.

- Also, keep in mind, a friend might get defensive at first when you raise the issue. Stay calm and friendly as you talk.

You may also help your friend by telling them about their ongoing patters. You need to work up the confidence to face the friend and tell him/her that certain behaviors are not okay. Prepare to give real examples and explain the consequences. Whichever the case, you do not have to participate in a hostile confrontation to pas your message. However, state clearly that you are not willing to be the fool in the story again.

- Instead of making potentially offensive comments such as " you are a liar" use some more tactful statements—" I think you it is not fair for you to twist my words whenever it suits you" Offensive statements will only make the friend shut down and not understand your argument.

- Remember that the manipulation cycle will continue unless you stand your ground and put a foot down.

Ignore the attempts of manipulative friends. Can you remember your grade school telling you that the best way to deal with someone who wronged you is to ignore them? Well, this principle also applies to manipulative people. Since a manipulative person will do the things he/she does to feel important, tuning him/her out is a sure way of disempowerment.

- This technique is best suited for those friends whose manipulative character shows occasionally. It is a civil way of ignoring what is not important and at the same time, retaining the friendship.

- Remember, a person can only control you as far as you allow him/her.

Stand your ground. When confronting a manipulative friend, it is important to stand your ground. A skilled manipulator will attempt to make you feel guilty and embarrassed; like you are at fault. He/she might accuse you of being insecure or jealous. Do not listen to the undeserved acts, rather, speak up when you are treated unfairly. You have a right to ask questions when someone is treating you unfairly.

- A manipulative friend will try to avoid this conversation. Look out for loopholes that the friend might use to change the topic such as acting as if the whole thing is a joke or undermining your feelings.

- If you are having a conversation about the behavior of your friend and he/she says "you are too sensitive" or "that's an overreaction" watch out. It might be another manipulation tactic. Keep in mind, you have every right to tell your friend when you are upset.

If you decide to end the friendship, check the advantages and disadvantages. Sometimes, the only option left to deal with manipulative friends is to end the relationship. For instance, if you have already explained to your friend that his/her behavior is not favorable and he/she fails to rectify, you will have to move on without them. Breaking off the friendship will not be an easy task especially if it has been there for years. However, you will be better off and happier in the long run. But before you pull the friendship plug; be sure of what you really want.

- When you have called the friendship off, your manipulative friend might use hurtful or childish tactics. For instance, he/she may spread rumors about you to your friends and acquaintances. Have the courage to ignore them. Picking a fight will only empower the slanderer. Again, such behaviors will only prove to you that the friend was not worth keeping.

- Finally, resist the temptation to spread rumors, slander or even fight with the former friend be the better person and walk

Chapter 14. Solutions to Overcome Manipulation

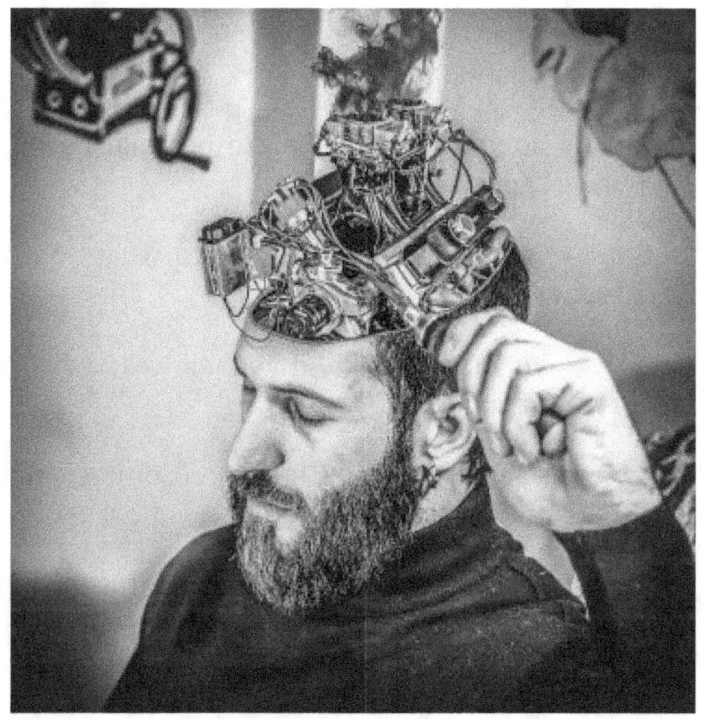

Cutting Off Manipulation Ties

This chapter is the climax of this book as you might be reading this chapter mainly because you have had enough of being manipulated or living with manipulative friends, family members, or your significant other. You might have reached the 'never again' point in your life after your bad experiences with manipulation. Getting long-lasting solutions to manipulation could end life's challenges and make the world a better place to live. Not every manipulative act leads to success, some lead to distress. Before solving any manipulative deeds, you need to ask yourself the following:

- After being manipulated, do you feel that you have been taken advantage of?

- Do you attempt to manipulate others?

- What are the reasons if you ever feel like manipulating others?

- Do you regret failing to be smarter once you have been manipulated?

- Can someone make you do what you do not want to do?

- Do you feel guilty if you fail to do what people request you to do?

- Do you feel angry, frustrated, or uncomfortable when around specific people?

This is not the best time to ask why manipulators manipulate others, but it is the best time to know that they will never do it again to you.

Consider a case where you desperately need attention from your friends mainly because your parents did not give it to you during your childhood. The attention could be sought from others because maybe your partner gives you none. In this case, you will have allowed people to manipulate you. You might fall for the appraisal quotes; being told how beautiful or handsome you are, how amazing and different you are, then you get manipulated in this kind of a fix. You will feel special and feel appreciated more than another person would.

If you are a victim of this, you must have reached your final straw with such kinds of manipulators and now, you need solutions.

You should avoid being desperate—This means that after every bad experience, you should never go seeking attention immediately. You should avoid any contact with a person, especially after being hurt as they may end up taking advantage of that and keep manipulating you.

When a deal sounds and appears too good, you should not give in immediately—This can be helpful especially in resisting some marketing manipulation tactics where sales persons try to persuade you to purchase a certain product that has been given subtle qualities, praised for its goodness, and how amazing it is. You should buy what you want without getting convinced to buy what you do not want.

Learn to control yourself even during flattery. Note that too much flattery can mean manipulation underway. Whenever people flirt too much or insist on getting a certain demand granted, always stop them immediately. Even if cooperation is good, it is bad at the same time as it can rub away your way of thinking.

You need to separate the 'truly needful people' in your life from those 'claiming to be in need' kind of people. There are people who genuinely need your help and those that you feel it is your responsibility or duty to help them. Such may include your child, aging parent, or a sick person. Then there are those that want to make you feel that their problem is your problem and their responsibilities are your responsibilities and that you are supposed to solve them. To sort out between a manipulator and a truly needful person, ask a friend or relative who is objective and cool. If they say 'No,' then that should be your response, too.

Manipulators can opt to be emotional to get what they want, as described in the manipulative techniques or ways on how to identify a manipulator. You should also learn how you should deal with emotional manipulation. You should note that:

It is of no use trying to be straightforward to an emotional manipulator. This is because every statement you make is always turned down. Consider the case below:

You: I am so disappointed; you forgot my birthday!

Your friend: It really makes me feel bad that you think I would by any chance forget your birthday. I wish I told you of the stress I have right now, but I did not want to stress you, too. I guess I should have valued your birthday, I am sorry.

In this case, your friend will even shed tears when responding. You will find yourself with nothing more to say and ending up babysitting your friend's angst. The solution to this is, trust your guts, senses, and instincts, do not take any apology or excuse that feels like nonsense.

An emotional persuader or manipulator always comes in the picture of a willing helper. Emotional manipulators will still agree to what you ask them to do for you. When you say, 'Thank you,' they reply with sighs and non-verbal cues that insinuates that they do not want to help you. When you question them, they will respond angrily and say you are unreasonable. The solution to this is avoiding challenging their sighs, make them accountable for their offer to help. Leave them to help and walk away to avoid these crazy dramas.

Do Not Entertain Them

In your relationships, you should never question your sanity or keep records for what was said or promised. A manipulator will turn things around and justify that they never gave any promises. These manipulators lie a lot, so that can make you even doubt your senses. Carry a notebook and start making notes after every conversation, claiming that you feel you are so forgetful and that they should not be worried about your craziness. This helps you remove yourself from their range and avoid manipulation.

When conditioned to act necessarily to decrease your guilty feelings, be on-the-know that you are getting manipulated. Manipulators make you feel guilty for almost everything; too much caring, loving, emotional, nurture, or support enough. Once you do anything for them, they never appreciate it and can even tell you that they did not expect whatever you did for them. You need to stop fighting other people's battles. Have a line to say to the manipulators who make you feel guilty. Tell them, 'I have great confidence to do this, do it your own.' Sit back and listen to their response; they probably lack one.

You should avoid people who cannot talk to you or deal with issues directly. They always let you know everything through their friends; they literally tend to send people to tell you what they want. Scream at them and never entertain any connections they send you.

When manipulators are angry, they tend to influence the environment and want everyone else to feel like them. They want to make people do things their way, by getting angry with everyone and expecting everyone to respond friendly. Remember, you also have your own psychological strains and needs, do not give in to such nonsense.

Anyone who is not accountable for their mess, no responsibility, and always complains about what other people do to them, is the kind of manipulators you should avoid with an immediate effect. You should never apologize for a mess that you are not responsible for. Leave the manipulator to realize their own mistakes and apologize appropriately. Avoid contact with the would-be manipulators. Just listen to them but act differently. They cannot hold you and force you to get manipulated anyway.

Setting personal boundaries can also be a long-lasting solution to manipulation. Before your relationship goes too far, and before anyone learns you in and out, set limits, then having to change in the midway. You can do so by stating the kind of behaviors you like or dislike. For instance, tell them they should not call you any time they feel like, mostly past 9 pm. Clearly define your goals so that it will be possible to know when you are getting manipulated. When you know your direction, it would be complicated for someone to influence you.

Be responsible and keep track of what you say or do. This helps you avoid getting blamed for other people's mistakes. Keep your notebook or computers safe from anybody else at work, school, or at home. People can access your information and defend themselves with it when they are accusing you.

Do not be emotional in every occasion. Your manipulators are waiting for this moment. They can easily manipulate you when you are emotionally down. Manipulators know how to twist the situation until they control you.

Differentiate manipulation from mental illness. Sounds funny, right? It can be a serious case, especially when manipulation becomes an everyday action. A manipulator cannot be independent, responsible, or accountable. Some of these conditions need proper treatment.

The truth hurts! Always hit any manipulator with the truth. Make their friends your enemies as this destroys their power base. By doing this, you will be a unique person that no one would want to mess around with.

Manipulation does not always entail other people manipulating you. You can as well be a manipulator, and hence, you need solutions on how to stop being a manipulator. Ask yourself whether you are a psychopath, a narcissist, aggressive, and any other characteristics of a manipulator. If you are not egotistical or you do not do anything centered at your own interests, then you are not a manipulator.

- Take time to know what you want

- Appreciate the honesty and avoid resenting people

- Learn to let go anything you cannot have; it is not the end of the world.

- Do not act out of defensiveness just because people turned down your requests. Embrace every response you get.

- Do not take everything too personal since this makes you feel powerless and end up manipulating others.

Manipulative people in society are meant to be ignored. Never correct them as this pulls you into their trap. You should know that guilt is a senseless emotion and that manipulators can make you feel the guilt of your mistakes or past. Do not compromise them. Stop doubting yourself and live your life appropriately. You need to feel good about yourself, be confident, and always be happy about your achievements. Appreciate and believe in what you are doing.

Chapter 15. Conclusion

Thank for making it through to the end of Manipulation, let's hope it was informative and able to provide you with all the tools you need to achieve your goals whatever they may be.

Manipulation is being used in every area of life, from TV to advertisements. While some forms might not be as cynical as others, manipulation in relationships and inter-personal relationships cause more problems than one might think. Equipped with the right tools, you can now spot manipulation and put an end to it before it harms you.

Since manipulation is so prevalent in our world, it's hard to avoid it altogether. But, keeping an eye and ear out can help you find those in your life that are more interested in their own needs and using you to get there.

Remember, don't allow yourself to stoop to their level. The best payback is to show them that you can live your own life without their influence. Burst their bubble when you see right through their manipulation tactics. That hurts them the most when they can't manipulate you to get what they want.

www.ingramcontent.com/pod-product-compliance
Lightning Source LLC
Chambersburg PA
CBHW071956070526
44583CB00015B/1221